GRANT, LEE, LINCOLN AND THE RADICALS

GRANT,
LEE,
LINCOLN
AND THE
RADICALS

Essays on **CIVIL WAR LEADERSHIP**

BRUCE CATTON
CHARLES P. ROLAND
DAVID DONALD
T. HARRY WILLIAMS

Edited, with a New Preface, by GRADY McWHINEY
With a New Introduction by JOSEPH T. GLATTHAAR

Louisiana State University Press
Baton Rouge

Louisiana Paperback Edition, 2001

10 09 08 07 06 05 04 03 02 01
5 4 3 2 1

Library of Congress Cataloging-in-Publication Data

Grant, Lee, Lincoln, and the Radicals : essays on Civil War leadership / Bruce Catton . . .
[et al.] ; edited, with a new preface, by Grady McWhiney ; with new introduction by
Joseph T. Glatthaar.
    p. cm.
Originally published: Evanston, Ill. : Northwestern University Press, 1964.
ISBN 0-8071-2742-6 (alk. paper)
    1. Grant, Ulysses S. (Ulysses Simpson), 1822–1885. 2. Lee, Robert E. (Robert
Edward), 1807–1870. 3. Lincoln, Abraham, 1809–1865. 4. Lincoln, Abraham,
1809–1865—Relations with radicals. 5. United States—History—Civil War,
1861–1865—Biography. 6. United States—History—Civil War, 1861–1865—
Campaigns. 7. Command of troops—History—19th century. 8. United
States—Politics and government—1861–1865. 9. Political leadership—United States
—History—19th century. 10. Radicals—United States—History—19th century.
I. McWhiney Grady.

E467 .G7 2001
973.7'092'2—dc21   2001038186

Contents

Preface to the Louisiana Paperback Edition

DURING THE FALL SEMESTER OF 1960, I arrived at Northwestern University in Evanston, Illinois, to teach the Civil War and other American history courses. I had recently received my Ph.D. from Columbia University, and everything seemed fine until after a few weeks I received a message to meet in the office of the university president, together with the graduate dean and the chair of my department. I answered the summons with anxiety. To my relief, I learned that I had not been brought before these high administrators to be censured or fired; they merely wanted me—in addition to teaching my regular classes—to organize and supervise a conference of history scholars, nonacademic experts, and enthusiasts to commemorate the American Civil War during its upcoming hundredth anniversary. Such an assignment both frightened and honored me. The president expressed his confidence in me and said he expected the celebration to be one in which the university could take pride. I would have funds and help from my colleagues and volunteers from the Civil War Round Table, an organization started in Chicago that grew into an international group of clubs dedicated to honoring and studying the American Civil War.

I realized that my colleagues, who knew little about the Civil War, would not be as helpful as I had hoped, but others were. I had my good friend E. B. "Pete" Long, a revered member of the Chicago Civil War Round Table, an accomplished Civil War writer, and later researcher for Bruce Catton. I asked Pete if Bruce might be interested in being one of our main speakers. Pete said he knew Bruce would be delighted. Sure enough, we soon had Catton on our symposium, speaking on General Ulysses S. Grant.

Finding someone to talk on Robert E. Lee was more difficult. His greatest biographer was no longer alive. Others might have been adequate, but I wanted someone who would defend Lee satisfactorily. The man I needed was professor Charles P. Roland of Tulane University, who had been teaching and completing his dissertation at Louisiana State University while I was there obtaining an M.A. I knew him well and was confident he would deliver an outstanding paper.

With fear and trepidation I asked two of the best scholars I knew, T. Harry Williams and David H. Donald, to join me for lunch at the Southern Historical Association meeting that November. I had studied with T. Harry at LSU, and David directed my dissertation at Columbia. To my delight they both accepted my invitation to speak at the symposium.

By the time the meeting was held, we knew that our superb speakers would fill an auditorium, and, collectively, create a volume of invaluable essays with new insights into the Civil War. It is gratifying that work done four decades ago has continued to hold an exciting and important place in Civil War historiography.

Texas Christian University   GRADY MCWHINEY

Introduction

JOSEPH T. GLATTHAAR

SOME THREE AND A HALF DECADES AGO, a handful of the most noted historians of the American Civil War gathered at Evanston, Illinois, on the campus of Northwestern University, to debate and commemorate the transforming event in our nation's past. Bruce Catton, Charles P. Roland, David Donald, and T. Harry Williams delivered papers, and they and other scholars argued and in some instances built consensus on potent issues of the war. Subsequently, the conference organizer, Dr. Grady McWhiney, published the four principal papers under the title *Grant, Lee, Lincoln and the Radicals.*

I first stumbled upon the thin little book in Fondren Library at Rice University while I was working on my master's degree. After flipping through it, I vowed to pick it up one day and devote to it the attention it seemed to merit. A couple of years later, I spotted it in the vast stacks of the State Historical Society of Wisconsin, and this time I devoured it with pleasure. Now, two decades later, it amazes me how pertinent these essays and their debates still are.

At a recent Civil War conference, John Y. Simon, editor of the *Papers of Ulysses S. Grant,* responded to a question from the audience about the best author on Grant. He suggested Bruce Catton as the most balanced and readable of all the Grant biographers. In this volume, Catton provides a wonderful, brief summary and assessment of Grant's Civil War career titled "The Generalship of Ulysses S. Grant." Catton contends that of all the United States Military Academy–trained officers, Grant adapted best to both the revolutionary nature of the Civil War and the mass armies composed of citizen soldiers. From the beginning, Grant realized that he must do more than place the opposing army at a disadvantage. A Union general must take the Rebel army apart, and the only way he could accomplish that was to fight it until it could fight no more. Catton also explains how Grant understood what made citizen soldiers tick. He was in tune with those who served under him and could therefore better utilize their talents and compensate for their weaknesses.

Catton does not hide Grant's warts. At Shiloh, the idea of an offensive so absorbed Grant that he overlooked the possibility of a Confederate counteroffensive. In the Overland Campaign of 1864, Grant may have underestimated the defensive prowess of seasoned troops, armed with rifled muskets and fighting behind fieldworks. Catton also chides Grant for a faulty command structure that left him and Meade in the field and Halleck behind in Washington. Yet Catton sees in Grant a touch of genius, especially at Vicksburg. Unlike many Civil War generals, Grant maintained the initiative, and in the end he compelled General Robert E. Lee to fight a war the Confederates could not win. The only significant element that is absent from this essay that more recent scholarship has developed is the Union's raiding strategy. All told, though, Catton's essay stands the test of time brilliantly.[1]

The second essay, "The Generalship of Robert E. Lee" by Charles P. Roland, is an extraordinary summary and assessment of the Confederate commander. Since the original presentation of this essay, Lee has come under attack from a host of historians. Some criticisms of Lee border on the ridiculous, the product of misused evidence or intellectual fantasy, but a number of the challenges are worthy of historical debate. Roland anticipates the current arguments or notes their antecedents and deftly disassembles them. What emerges is the finest brief essay on Lee that exists today.[2]

Roland assesses Lee by means of a largely overlooked truism: A general's record must be weighed against the resources at his command.

Lee, like other Confederate generals, fought the war with major manpower shortages, an inadequate and declining rail network that largely negated the advantage of interior lines, profound localist views among both the Confederate populace and its politicians, and the increasingly troublesome institution of slavery. Rather than acting as an eighteenth-century leader or as a follower of Jomini, Lee comported himself, in Roland's view, as someone whose approach to warfare mirrored the opinions of the Prussian theorist Carl von Clausewitz. When a general lacks the resources to destroy the enemy's armed forces, Clausewitz argues that he must resort to other means, as Lee did by threatening to seize the northern capital or inflicting casualties beyond expectations to weaken his opponent's will.

Although Lee held overall command only in the waning days of the war, critics have challenged him for parochial views. Roland rebuts that argument by depicting Lee as someone who acted deferentially to his commander in chief, but who provided President Jefferson Davis with sound advice on a host of subjects. Lee proposed a strategy for the entire Confederacy in 1863, even though he had no authority, calling for simultaneous offensives, just as Grant did in 1864. Early on, he advised Davis to adopt conscription, and he recommended that the Confederacy employ African Americans as soldiers and give freedom as a reward for that service.

The Lee who emerges in these pages is one who blends intellect with audacity, a farsighted and brilliant military commander who got into the mind of his opponent. Throughout the war, Lee was sensitive to the needs and concerns of civilians. He used his powerful, mobile army in Northern Virginia to protect the governmental and industrial center of Richmond and to threaten the North, which kept Union leadership off balance and prevented effective concentration until the end of the war. Whether on the offensive or defensive, he fought superbly, and against tremendous odds. In fact, Roland explains, if Lee had a fault it was that he gave subordinates wide latitude, when some required more precise direction than others.

Just as the Lee who emerges from these pages is one for the ages, so Roland's depiction of him has stood the test of time. Only Jay Luvaas's exceptional essay "Lee and the Operational Art," published in *Parameters* in 1992, offers a new and valuable perspective on Lee as a military commander. [3]

While Catton and Roland assess their subjects in very favorable terms, they do so without diminishing the competence of the principal opposing commander. Despite the passage of nearly four decades, these brief works still form much of the framework for debate on political reconstruction on the national level today.

In "Devils Facing Zionwards," Donald challenges the standing view of the Radicals at war with Lincoln, which Williams originally proposed in his 1941 book *Lincoln and the Radicals*. Donald argues that scholars must place the Radicals in better context. During the war years, Radicals voted in concert with fellow Republicans, taking bold steps to end slavery. At times when congressional views differed from those of Lincoln, Radicals also had the support of most conservative Republicans. The problem with most assessments of the Radicals, Donald insists, is that historians start with the premise that Lincoln's program was sound. They have difficulty accepting the idea that criticism of the president's policies stemmed from belief in genuine and intelligent alternatives, or from disappointment with the way the administration mishandled matters. Scholars, he counsels, must view the administration as did informed northerners in that day. [4]

Donald does not see the Radicals as a unified bloc during the war years, but rather as a group that solidified in opposition to President Andrew Johnson's policies. While he admits that some Radicals launched vituperative attacks against Lincoln, Democrats had challenged Presidents Franklin Pierce and James Buchanan with equal furor. The Republican party, he reminds us, was a coalition of state parties, with powerful local interests and rivalries at work. Old rivalries between Whigs and Democrats underlay many Republican divisions and were the basis for vociferous attacks.

In his essay "Lincoln and the Radicals," Williams asserts that consensus historians have tried to depict the Radicals' behavior as normal political infighting. In his view, Radicals were doctrinaire and dogmatic, seeking more than just the absolute destruction of slavery; they also sought to punish those who supported it. They were a righteous lot who paid little heed to consequences.

While Donald attempts to place the Radicals in the larger context of mid-nineteenth-century politics, Williams reminds us that these were no normal times. In these days of great national crisis, Williams feels, the Radicals should have united with fellow Republicans. Instead, they formed the Committee on the Conduct of the War in a bold and unprecedented attempt by Congress to dominate policy. Ultimately, Radicals fell in line with Lincoln for the election of 1864, but only because a savvy Lincoln had outmaneuvered them and they had no alternative.

Since the publication of Donald's and Williams's essays, scholarship has staked a claim between their guideposts, though much closer to Donald's position. In his classic study *Free Soil, Free Labor, Free Men,* Eric Foner agrees with the two scholars that opposition to slavery united all Republicans, but he establishes, in addition to Radicals and Conservatives, a third camp among them, the Moderates, to which Foner designates Lincoln. Hans Trefousse in *Radical Republicans,* which has supplanted Williams's for the best book on the subject, finds that Lincoln got along much better with the Radicals than Williams claimed. Where Williams discovered largely conflict, Trefousse sees more cooperation and consensus. Allan G. Bogue, whose careful quantitative study has helped us determine who the Radicals were, entitled his great book on the Radicals in the Senate *The Earnest Men,* reflecting Donald's softer perspective. Yet recent scholarship on the Committee on the Conduct of the War by Bruce Tap has reaffirmed Williams's basic conclusions about that body's maneuvers and manipulations. Perhaps the pendulum has begun to shift back toward Williams. [5]

In sum, *Grant, Lee, Lincoln and the Radicals* is an outstanding collection of short essays that have withstood the test of time. After nearly four decades, they still shape and illuminate our debate on the central figures of this tempestuous period in our nation's history. Anyone interested in the Civil War should find a space in their collection for it.

NOTES

1. For information on strategy, see Herman Hattaway and Archer Jones, *How the North Won the Civil War: A Military History of the Civil War* (Urbana: University of Illinois Press, 1983); Archer Jones, *Civil War Command and Strategy: The Process of Victory and Defeat* (New York: The Free Press, 1992); Joseph T. Glatthaar, *Partners in Command: Relationships Between Leaders in the Civil War* (New York: The Free Press, 1994).

2. For a couple of books that criticize Lee, see J. F. C. Fuller, *Grant and Lee: A Study in Personality and Generalship* (Bloomington: Indiana University Press, 1957), which is the best of the original criticisms; Thomas L. Connelly, *The Marble Man: Robert E. Lee and His Image in American Society* (Baton Rouge: Louisiana State University Press, 1977); Alan T. Nolan, *Lee Reconsidered: General Robert E. Lee and Civil War History* (Chapel Hill: University of North Carolina Press, 1991).

3. Jay Luvaas, "Lee and the Operational Art," *Parameters* (Autumn 1992), 2–18.

4. T. Harry Williams, *Lincoln and the Radicals* (Madison: University of Wisconsin Press, 1941); David Donald, *Lincoln Reconsidered: Essays on the Civil War* (New York: Alfred A. Knopf, 1947).

5. Eric Foner, *Free Soil, Free Labor, Free Men: The Ideology of the Republican Party Before the Civil War* (New York: Oxford University Press, 1970); Hans L. Trefousse, *The Radical Republicans: Lincoln's Vanguard for Racial Justice* (New York: Alfred A. Knopf, 1969); Bruce Tap, *Over Lincoln's Shoulder: The Committee on the Conduct of the War* (Lawrence: University Press of Kansas, 1998); Allan G. Bogue, *The Earnest Men: Republicans of the Civil War Senate* (Ithaca: Cornell University Press, 1981); Allan G. Bogue, *The Congressman's Civil War* (Cambridge: Cambridge University Press, 1989).

Preface

THERE ARE MORE Civil War controversies than there were battles between 1861 and 1865. All of the major figures and events, and most of the minor ones, have been interpreted and reinterpreted, praised and damned. Some of the controversies are inconsequential; others are so important that their resolution would necessitate the rewriting of a large part of American history.

Two of the most significant Civil War disputes are over the generalship of Ulysses S. Grant and Robert E. Lee, and the political leadership of Abraham Lincoln. Was Grant or Lee the better general, and why? What forces—personal, social, economic, political, and military—influenced their actions? Was either of them a revolutionary military thinker, a tactical or strategic innovator? Was Grant a "modern" general? Did his ignorance of Jomini and other military writers free Grant from obsolete concepts of war? Was Lee too committed to textbooks? Did his military education and conservative Virginia background make him inflexible? Was Lincoln a great war leader, or an inept blunderer? Did he hold his party together, or drive it apart? Were his policies radical, or conservative? What was his relationship with the Radical Republicans, and who were they?

These are some of the questions about Grant, Lee, and Lincoln that divide historians. No serious Civil War student can avoid these issues, for they shape every interpretation of the 1860's. Moreover, such controversies are a necessary part of the historical process of examination and re-examination; they have produced many of the fresh theses and new insights into the Civil War.

To present the latest thought and research on Grant, Lee, and Lincoln, Northwestern University invited a number of distinguished scholars to participate in a Civil War Centennial Symposium. The four papers read at this forum are included in this volume. Each essay is a major contribution to an understanding of the Civil War.

My colleagues and I are grateful to Bruce Catton, Charles P. Roland, David Donald, and T. Harry Williams for brilliant appraisals of their subjects. We also thank those able historians—James I. Robertson, Jr., Ralph G. Newman, Paul M. Angle, and Bernard A. Weisberger—who criticized the principal papers; President J. Roscoe Miller of Northwestern University, whose interest and support made the symposium possible; the Civil War Centennial Commission, for honoring the symposium with the Commission's Certificate of Achievement; and the Graduate School of Northwestern University and Dean Moody E. Prior, whose support has contributed to the publication of this volume.

I am personally indebted to many members of the Northwestern faculty and staff for their contributions to the symposium's success. My special thanks to Gray C. Boyce, Richard W. Leopold, Ray A. Billington, Clarence L. Ver Steeg, and Robert H. Wiebe.

Northwestern University   GRADY MCWHINEY

GRANT, LEE, LINCOLN AND THE RADICALS

The Generalship of Ulysses S. Grant

by BRUCE CATTON

THE AMERICAN CIVIL WAR confronted the professional soldier with a vexing series of problems which went far beyond anything he could possibly have been expected to learn at West Point.

West Point gave its graduates a first-rate training, but it told them very little about some of the things that would be required of them in the 1860's. It had trained them for a different sort of war altogether—for a war of professionals, with set rules, established values and recognized limits—and the very fact that it had trained them well and thoroughly meant that they were apt to find themselves bewildered once the nation thrust them into a war which made up its own rules as it went along, groped blindly toward values which had never been defined, and came in the end to recognize no limits whatsoever.

For the Civil War resembled war as set forth in the textbooks only to an extent. It was, to begin with, what its traditional name says it was—a civil war, not a war with some foreign nation—and it contained elements West Point had never dreamed of. It had to be fought by citizen-soldiers drawn from a land which might be exceedingly pugnacious but which had an immense impatience with restraints and formalities. Problems of politics and of economics were woven through every part of its fabric. The techniques of a newly mechanized age had to be taken into account. On top of everything, it was on both sides a war of the people, whose imperious and often impatient desires exerted a constant pressure which no general could ignore.

To appraise the generalship of any of the great soldiers in

that war, therefore, it is necessary to understand first just what it was that the Civil War required of them. It required straight military competence, to be sure, and those indefinable qualities of leadership which professional training may develop but cannot implant; but it also called for a great adaptability, a readiness to find unorthodox solutions for unorthodox problems, an understanding of just what it was that the American people were trying to do in that terrible war they were waging with themselves.

Now the first thing to take into consideration here is that the American Civil War was—or became, not long after it had begun—an all-out war; which means that it was essentially quite unlike the kind of war professional soldiers of the mid-nineteenth century usually had in mind.

Each side was fighting for an absolute; to compromise was to lose. The South was fighting for independence, the North for reunion. Inextricably interwoven with these opposing causes was the matter of chattel slavery. The men of each side, in other words, came at an early stage to believe passionately that they were fighting both for national survival and for human freedom —the Southerner, for his own personal freedom, the Northerner, for freedom in the abstract, but both for freedom. Each side, accordingly, believed that it was fighting for a high and holy cause and that final victory was worth any conceivable sacrifice. Victory was more important than anything else. What it cost did not matter, and what it would finally mean could be settled later on; while the war lasted victory would be pursued with immense singleness of purpose. And to drive for absolute victory is of course to wage all-out war in the modern manner.[1]

Now this was not what most professional soldiers of that era had in mind at all. They had been brought up in a doctrine that came down from the eighteenth century. Wars were usually fought for limited objectives, and they were fought in a limited way; they were primarily matters for the armies, and they were conducted up to the point where they began to cost more than they were likely to be worth, at which point they were brought to an end. The settlement that finally ended a war was of course a matter for governments to determine, not for generals; what the generals had to remember was that sooner or later there would be some sort of settlement, and that until the settlement was made it was wise to conduct affairs without causing too much breakage.

This meant that wars had to a certain extent become formalized. They were in a way like immense chess games, performed with intricate maneuvers that followed the book; going by the book, a good general always knew when he was licked, and behaved accordingly. One of the most cerebral and highly educated of Northern soldiers, General Don Carlos Buell, told the court of inquiry which considered his case after he had been removed from the command of the Army of the Cumberland that it ought to be quite possible to conduct an entire campaign successfully without fighting a single battle.[2] Make the right moves and you will win: you do not need to be especially combative, but you must be very careful, leaving as little as possible to chance, never moving until everything is ready, making those maneuvers and occupying those strategic points which will finally persuade your opponent that he has been beaten.

This attitude formed part of the mental background of a great many of the professional soldiers who were given important assignments in the early part of the Civil War, and it was precisely this attitude which kept some of them from being successful. This, to repeat, was a different kind of war. The two sides which were involved were not going to quit until somebody made them quit. Victories would go, not to the man who followed the book faithfully, but to the man who was willing and able to get in close and slug until something broke. He would, to be sure, need a good deal of professional ability to get in close and to slug effectively after he got there, but his ultimate objective was, quite simply, the enemy's will and ability to resist. Until he broke that he accomplished nothing.

This requirement rested with particular weight on the Federal generals. The Southerner had one thing working for him: it was always conceivable that even if he did not actually win he could compel the Northerner to give up the fight from sheer war weariness. The Northerner had no similar reliance. He would get no final victory unless Confederate strength was utterly destroyed. He had to be aggressive, because a stalemate would work in favor of his opponent. Whether he realized the fact or not, the Federal soldier was fighting to enforce an unconditional surrender. It was his task, not merely to compel his foe to come to terms, but to obliterate a nation.

It was not easy for the average professional soldier to grasp this point, and a number of good men never got an inkling of it. It is perhaps significant that the three Federal generals who most often were called "brilliant" by their Old Army associates —Buell, McClellan, and Halleck—were men who failed utterly to see this requirement and who accordingly never measured up to the high expectations which had been made regarding them. These men had studied the science of war with great care, and they brought keen intelligence to the task. Their trouble was that the Civil War called on them for qualities which their studies had never revealed to them. In his statement that it should be possible to win a campaign without actually fighting a battle, Buell was entirely correct—by the book. But the book did not apply in his case, because his assignment in Kentucky and Tennessee could not be discharged as long as the Confederate Army of Tennessee remained in existence. It was not enough for him to put it at a disadvantage. He had to take it apart, and he could not conceivably do that without compelling it to fight until it could fight no more.

In the same way, Halleck completely missed his opportunity

after the battle of Shiloh and the fall of Corinth in the spring of 1862. He had assembled an army of perhaps 125,000 men in northern Mississippi, and to oppose him Beauregard had substantially fewer than half that many men. With the light of after-knowledge it is easy to see that Halleck ought to have pressed his advantage to the utmost, driving his foe on relentlessly and compelling him at last to fight a battle that could only result in annihilation. Instead, Halleck went by the book. He undertook to occupy territory, dividing his army into detachments, leisurely setting to work to consolidate his advantages; he saw the map, and the things which a strategist ought to do on it, rather than the men in arms who carried the opposing nation on the points of their bayonets. Behaving thus, he gave the Confederacy a breathing spell in which it assembled new levies, dug in to resist a new Federal offensive, and in the end took the initiative away from him and marched north almost to the Ohio River. The war went on for two more years.

Another responsibility rested on men in the Federal high command. The Federal government has almost overwhelming advantages in the Civil War, from the beginning to the end. In manpower, in money, in raw materials and manufacturing capacity, in access to world markets, in the ability to raise, feed, equip, and transport armies—in all of the things that go to make up military capacity in time of war—the resources of the North so far overshadowed those of the South that one is compelled at times to wonder what ever made the leaders of the Confederacy think that they could possibly win. This enormous advantage was bound to bring victory, in the end, if it could just be applied steadily, remorselessly and without a break, and it was above all other things up to the Federal generals to see this and to govern themselves accordingly. They had, in other words, the ability to apply and maintain a pressure which the Confederacy could not hope to resist. They could afford mistakes, they could afford wastage, they could afford almost anything except the failure to make constant use of the power that was available to them.

It was just here, perhaps, that the reality of the Civil War departed most completely from the orthodox military tradition. Two very different economic and social systems were struggling for survival. One of them was fitted to win such a struggle if it went to the limit, and the other, the weaker system, was not. In effect, a Confederate leader had his own army to rely on and nothing more; the Federal leader had not only his own army but the infinite war-potential of a rich, populous, highly organized industrial state. "Brilliance" in the purely military field was the reliance of the Southern soldier—possibly his only reliance—as Robert E. Lee abundantly demonstrated; the Northerner's reliance was something quite different, calling not so much for an understanding of the rules of war as for an understanding of the ways by which a great nation enforces its will.

Along with everything else this required the Northern general to give a certain amount of thought to the institution of chattel slavery, simply because the slave system was one of the main props—perhaps the most important one of all—for the Southern economy which was the ultimate support of Southern armies. This prop, while important, was exceedingly fragile. One of the facts that had driven slave-state leaders to secession in the first place had been the dawning realization that the peculiar institution could continue to exist only if it were carefully protected against all outside interference. A general who took a hostile army into slave territory was providing such interference, whether he meant to or not. Regardless of his own feelings in respect to slavery, the peculiar institution became of necessity one of his military objectives. He was fighting, to repeat, a total war, and in a total war the enemy's economy is to be undermined in any way possible. Slavery was the southern economy's most vulnerable spot, and a Northern general could not be neutral in respect to it. Every time one of his soldiers extracted a plantation hand from bondage—every time the mere presence of his army disorganized the slave-labor system in its area and caused a blind exodus of men and women from the huddled slave cabins—he was helping to disarm the Confederacy.

It must be confessed that the Northern general was under certain handicaps during the first year and one-half of the struggle. Up to the fall of 1862, it was official government policy that the war was being fought solely to restore the Union, and generals were instructed not to campaign against slavery. This, to be sure, was a vain hope, but generals were supposed to follow top policy even when it was impossible; and this policy could not be followed, simply because the private soldiers took things into their own hands. The soldiers quickly came to equate the possession of slaves with opposition to the Union. In places like Kentucky this often led them to despoil the property of men who were stoutly Unionist in their leanings, but there was no help for it. Regardless of what the generals might say, the private Federal soldier was predominantly an emancipationist whenever he got south, not because he himself had any especial feelings against slavery but simply because he realized that slavery supported the nation he was fighting against.

Slavery, indeed, was the one institution which could not possibly survive an all-out war. A Union general might deplore this fact, but he was obliged to take it into account. Here, in short, was one more extremely important field in which the professional soldier's training and traditions were of no use to him. He had to understand what made his country tick, and in the long run what he did had to be done in the light of that understanding. There was nothing in the textbooks to help him. Like the men he commanded, the general had to have a good deal of the citizen-soldier in him.

It is sometimes said, indeed, that the most successful generals in the Civil War were men who had left the army in the prewar years and had had experience in the civilian world. This is only partly true. It applies to such men as Grant and Sherman, to be sure, but it does not apply at all to men like Lee, Joseph E. Johnston, Stonewall Jackson, and George Thomas, who had never been or wanted to be anything but professional soldiers; and one of the men who most faithfully tried to make war by the old tradition was a man who had left the army and had had a highly successful career in business—George B. McClellan. Yet one is bound to feel that particularly on the Northern side a man who had had some experience outside of the army might have gained something from it. The war had strong non-professional aspects, and an officer who had something of a non-professional viewpoint—who had learned, by first-hand experience, something about the way the American people go about their business and try to make their will felt—could derive an advantage from that fact.

I suggest that it is only against this background that we can intelligently evaluate the generalship of the man under whom the Federal armies finally won the Civil War—Ulysses S. Grant.

Grant first comes on the wartime stage in the fall of 1861, at Cairo, Illinois, where he commanded a body of troops which would presently be used in the attempt to open the Mississippi Valley. It is possible to see, even before this first campaign got under way, some of his essential qualities: an uncomplicated belief in direct action, a realization of the things that could be done with raw troops, and a constant desire to strike for complete victory rather than for the attainment of a minor advantage.

In September, 1861, Grant commanded approximately 15,-000 men. All of his men—like all of the other men in Union and Confederate armies at that time—were poorly trained and poorly armed, but he wanted to use them at once. He told his chief of staff, John A. Rawlins, that when two unprepared armies faced one another, the commander of one of those armies would gain very little by waiting until his troops were thoroughly prepared. This, said Grant, simply meant that his opponent would have time to do the same thing, and in the end the relative strengths of the opposing armies would be about what they had been at the start.[3] It might be noted that in expressing this opinion Grant was departing from military orthodoxy. The professional soldier had a natural distaste for trying to make a campaign with an army whose training, discipline, and equipment were deficient, and the shambling assemblages of newly uniformed young men who made up the armies in the fall of 1861 had deficiencies too obvious to overlook. The disaster at Bull Run simply underlined the point. In his ability to see that the other side was equally handicapped, Grant was being definitely unprofessional. His attitude here was much more the attitude of the civilian than of the trained soldier; he was quite willing to use an imperfect instrument, provided that his opponent's instrument was equally imperfect.

And so Grant, that fall, wanted to attack the Confederate stronghold at Columbus, on the Mississippi River. He knew that his troops were by no means ready to confront a trained, tightly organized army, but he knew also that they were not going to have to confront anything of the kind. The army they would fight was in no better shape than themselves. Under the circumstances, Grant wanted to fight as soon as possible.

There is of course another side to this argument, and Grant doubtless got a certain amount of enlightenment from his first battle, the sharp engagement fought at Belmont, across the river from Columbus. Here Grant attacked a Confederate force and drove it from the field in temporary rout, which was just what he had expected to do. What he had not anticipated was the fact that his unready troops fell into complete disorder because they had won a victory. They got out of hand, wandered about looting the Confederate camp, listening to spread-eagle speeches by their colonels, and in general acting as if the battle was over. The Confederates across the river sent over fresh troops, and Grant's men in turn were driven off in rout, escaping final disaster only because Grant managed at last to get them back to their transports and take them up the river to safety. Because they were so imperfectly disciplined and organized, they had lost a victory which they had won.[4]

Grant's original idea, in other words, needed to be toned down slightly. But it did have some merit, and it went hand in hand with another notion, equally repugnant to military orthodoxy. Not long after Belmont, it was suggested to Grant that by proper maneuvering he could compel the Confederates to evacuate that stronghold at Columbus. Grant dissented vigorously. There was (he insisted) very little point in merely compelling the enemy's army to retreat; sooner or later that army would have to be fought, when it was fought it would have to be destroyed outright—dispersed in open combat, or hemmed in and captured lock, stock and barrel—and this might as well be done at once.[5] Making the enemy retreat simply postponed the showdown that had to come eventually.

The big business, in short, was to fight, to fight all-out, and to win the most decisive victory imaginable. There was no point in a campaign for limited objectives. Any battle which left the opposing army on its feet and breathing struck General Grant as imperfect.

It is a little surprising to find a Federal general feeling this way in the fall of 1861. The war then was still young, and the Northern government was still trying, with much fumbling and inefficiency, to get its strength organized. The lesson taught by Bull Run—that it was folly to try to make a campaign with an unprepared army—was still fresh in every man's mind. Autumn of 1861 was a time to get ready. Decisive action would have to come later.

But it is just possible, in spite of Belmont, that the Bull Run lesson had been learned a little too well. In Missouri, both Sterling Price and Nathaniel Lyon had demonstrated that great things could be done with the most grotesquely unready armies if the man in charge insisted on it. The Bull Run lesson needed to be interpreted in the light of two additional facts, which were not readily recognizable to the average professional. First, every Federal army, no matter how much it lacked in the way of training and equipment, was at least as well off in those respects as the army it was going to have to fight. Second, the Federal side did have an immense advantage in numbers, in war material, and in the capacity to make its losses good. That advantage was just as genuine an asset in the fall of 1861 as it was in the spring of 1864. It needed to be used.

It was used, presently, beginning in January, 1862, and what happened thereafter is instructive.

Albert Sidney Johnston, who commanded for the Confederates in the western theater, did not have nearly enough men to defend the long line that ran from the Mississippi River to the Cumberland Plateau, and he had held his ground throughout the fall simply by a skillful bluff which made his strength look much greater than it was.[6] When Grant and his naval coadjutor, Flag Officer Andrew Foote, insisted that this line be attacked at the earliest possible date they were simply reacting to a subconscious knowledge of that fact, and between the two of them they apparently persuaded the authorities to open an offensive a little ahead of time. So Foote's gunboats promptly knocked off Fort Henry, on the Tennessee—and Johnston's whole line immediately collapsed. (For the record, of course, it should be noted that George H. Thomas had already broken the eastern anchor of the line by winning the battle of Mill Springs, or Logan's Cross Roads, in Kentucky.) Grant drove on to capture Fort Donelson, and Johnston could do nothing but order an immediate retreat and try to regroup in northern Mississippi.

Note that the driving force in this whole campaign came from Grant. His superior officer, General Halleck, was obviously drawn into the campaign before he was quite ready; and General Buell, who commanded for the Federals east of the Tennessee River, went into action with even greater reluctance, protesting that the thing had not been properly prepared for and complaining bitterly because Grant forced the occupation of Nashville before Buell was ready for it. It was Grant, also, who believed that this victory ought to be followed up with speed. Halleck restrained him—we must pause in order to get everything arranged properly, there must be due thought for reinforcements and lines of supply, it would be most risky to go plunging on before everybody is ready—and, as a result, the advance up the defenseless Tennessee was made with much caution. In the end Johnston was given seven weeks, which he did not really need to be given, in order to bring his scattered forces together at Corinth. Johnston used the time to good advantage, and at Shiloh he struck a blow which nearly redressed the balance.[7]

Admittedly, Shiloh does not show Grant at his best. He displayed here the defects of his qualities. Eager to press the advantage and overwhelm a beaten enemy, he thought so much about the delayed offensive that he apparently overlooked the fact that his enemy might launch a counteroffensive. When at last he was allowed to advance he advanced incautiously, and Johnston's massive counterstroke hit him before he was quite ready. The near-debacle at Pittsburg Landing needs to be interpreted in the light of the fact that if Grant had had his way the Federal army would have been ready to move forward from that bleak highland three weeks before the battle actually took place, at which time Johnston would have been in no shape to make an effective defense.

One more point needs to be made about Shiloh, and it highlights one more of Grant's characteristic traits. In the first day's fight, Grant's army unquestionably was defeated: but Grant himself was not defeated at all. Unforgettable, to any student of the battle, is General Sherman's account of meeting Grant at midnight, in the rain, after the first day's fight had ended. Grant was standing under a tree, keeping as dry as he could, puffing a cigar; Sherman came up to him, believing that the only possible course was to order a retreat the next morning, and said something to the effect that the day had been very tough and had gone badly. Grant nodded, bit his cigar, drew on it briefly, and then said: "Yes. Beat 'em in the morning, though." Grant, in other words, hung on, waited for Buell and Wallace to reinforce him, refused to think of withdrawal, made his counterattack on the second day, and in the end won one of the most significant Union victories of the entire war. After Shiloh, the Confederates in the west were doomed to a losing defensive.

Shiloh's gains, once more, were partly nullified by Halleck's caution. Halleck came on the scene a few days after the battle. He brought heavy reinforcements, so that before long the Federal army in northern Mississippi totaled approximately 125,-000 men: Beauregard, commanding for the Confederates after Albert Sidney Johnston's battle death, had a scant 50,000. Halleck's army could have gone anywhere it chose. The heart of the South was open, and Beauregard could not conceivably have made a stand-up fight in opposition. But Halleck was a cautious, careful professional, a man who knew war by the book rather than by reality. He knew that Shiloh had almost been a disaster because the Federals had been incautious and had not had their defenses ready. In his advance, Halleck would not make that mistake.

He edged forward with painstaking care, taking upward of a month to make a 30-mile advance, and when Beauregard at last evacuated Corinth and retreated—there was nothing else Beauregard could possibly have done—Halleck split his forces into segments, devoting himself to the occupation of "strategic points," to the protection and repair of railroad lines, to the consolidation of his position. The great opportunity was missed. The Confederates were even able before the summer was out to put on a counteroffensive, which saw a Confederate army go nearly to the Ohio River; to this day no one knows quite what that stroke might have accomplished if it had been commanded by anyone other than Braxton Bragg. The driving offensive spirit which Grant gave his army evaporated once Halleck got on the scene, and in consequence the Federal move to open the Mississippi could not be resumed until nearly the end of 1862.

Grant's Mississippi campaign, from its unhappy beginning at Holly Spring to the final surrender of Pemberton's army at Vicksburg on July 4, 1863, was of course one of the decisive strokes of the war—and one of the most brilliant. It is interesting here simply because it shows Grant in a somewhat unfamiliar guise. His movement downstream from Milliken's Bend, his crossing of the river, his lightning campaign to Jackson and back via Champion Hill to Vicksburg, his ability to herd Pemberton into the isolated fortress and to keep the Confederate relieving column under Joe Johnston at arm's length until Pemberton at last had to give up—this was one of the most dazzling campaigns of the entire war. It is interesting to note that in its beginning, at least, Grant did not have an advantage in numbers. When he crossed the river, cut loose from his base and marched into the interior, there were actually more Confederates than Unionists in Mississippi. The hoary assertion that Grant won victories simply because the odds were always heavily in his favor collapses here. This was a campaign in the Stonewall Jackson manner—great daring, fast and deceptive movement, hard blows struck at fragments of the opposing forces, ending in a victory which went far to determine the outcome of the entire war.

Whatever else it may have been, this campaign was not the

campaign of a dull, unimaginative man who was a simple slugger and nothing more. Military genius was at work here. The Grant of the Vicksburg campaign was one of the great captains.

To midsummer of 1863, in other words, Grant's record is in the main excellent. He has carried out his assignments, learning his grim trade as he goes along, guided always by the offensive spirit, discovering along the way (at a high cost, admittedly) that the offensive needs to be leavened with a certain amount of caution; he has swallowed two opposing armies whole, he has opened the Mississippi Valley to the Union, and he has abundantly justified his belief that a Union general needs to apply the pressure to the Union's foes without a letup. It has worked. The war, as far as the Union is concerned, is over the peak.

The Chattanooga campaign, interesting as it is, must be recognized as more or less incidental. At Chattanooga Grant was called on to do little more than pick up the pieces which had been dropped at the disastrous battle of Chickamauga. Grant took charge at Chattanooga at a time when the Union army had escaped the immediate threat of capture, which loomed so large immediately after the retreat from Chickamauga. All that was needed was a cool, unhurried, business-like grasp of the situation and a determination to break out of the besieging ring as soon as everything was ready. This much Grant provided; it is extremely probable that George H. Thomas, left to himself, would have provided it equally well, and although at the time Grant's victory at Chattanooga struck Northerners as a superlative achievement the victory must be written down simply as one which any competent Northern commander would have won under similar circumstances. Probably Grant's matter-of-fact, common-sense coolness was his chief asset here.

After Chattanooga, Grant's elevation to supreme command was inevitable. The step came early in the spring of 1864, when Grant was commissioned lieutenant-general and was entrusted with the conduct of the nation's whole military effort. All that had gone before was preparation; now came the great challenge, the unlimited responsibility, the final time of testing. Any appraisal of Grant's qualities as a soldier must finally rest on what he did after the supreme command was given to him.

What Grant did, beginning in the spring of 1864, was by no means confined to Virginia. He stayed in Virginia, to be sure, and the army that fought against Robert E. Lee was known —against logic, and against military reality—as "Grant's Army"; but the whole war was Grant's, and what happened in Tennessee and in Georgia, and elsewhere, was Grant's responsibility. And critiques of Grant's military capacity can grow a little foggy here, because the critic runs the danger of succumbing to one of two oversimplifications.

The first one can be stated thus: Grant was responsible for the grand strategy of the final year, the war was at last won, and Grant therefore is a great soldier.

The other goes off in the opposite direction: Grant fought against Lee with an overwhelming advantage in numbers, took frightful losses, was never able to beat Lee in the open field, won at last because he did have that advantage in numbers, and hence was simply a slugger who came at last to victory because under the circumstances he could hardly have come to anything else.

There is an element of truth in each oversimplification. Neither one offers a proper evaluation of Grant's capacity. Each one needs to be examined closely, and the two finally need to be blended together.

It is entirely true that the grand strategy of the final year, which worked, was Grant's. The war was not simply Virginia; the western theater was part of it, too. Sherman's armies moved remorselessly into the deep South, disemboweling the Confederacy, making it incapable of firm resistance, reducing that tragically beset nation to nothing more than the territory between Richmond, Virginia, and Raleigh, North Carolina, while still other armies mopped up the outlying territories. This concept was Grant's, and the responsibility was his. (If Sherman's bold march from Atlanta to the sea had gone sour and had resulted in a lost army and a fatal setback to the Union cause, the man who would have had to shoulder the blame was Grant.) When 1864 began, the Confederacy lived because of two armies —the Army of Northern Virginia under Lee, and the Army of Tennessee, under Johnston. (There were other, lesser armies elsewhere, but they were peripheral.) As long as these two armies lived, the Confederacy would live; when they were destroyed the Confederacy would die. It was Grant who made those two armies the principal objectives for the Federal war effort; it was Grant who saw to it that the force needed to destroy those armies was mustered, supported, and relentlessly applied. If the grand strategy of the war's final year worked, Grant is the man who is entitled to take the bow. He had the authority to do these things, and he used it up to the hilt. The result was victory.

At the same time, Grant's conduct of the campaign in Virginia is extremely relevant to any appraisal of his abilities, and it is clear that this campaign did not go quite as Grant had hoped that it would go. His real aim when he planned the campaign was neither to capture Richmond nor to force the Confederate army into retreat; it was simply to destroy that army, and he hoped that he would be able to do it fairly quickly. Grant suspected, when he came east, that the Federal Army of the Potomac had somehow never been made to fight all-out. It had capacities, he believed, that had not quite been called on; he would call on them to the limit, and by unremitting aggressiveness would compel Lee to make a stand-up fight in which the superior Federal advantages in manpower and materiel would quickly win a decisive victory.

This, of course, did not happen. The campaign lasted very nearly a year, it was enormously costly to the Union army, and in the end it succeeded largely because the North could endure a long process of attrition better than the South could. Grant did not do what he set out to do; what he had been able to do against other Confederate commanders in the west he was not able to do against Lee. The long series of wearing, hideously expensive battles which in a few months almost destroyed the old fighting capacity of the Army of the Potomac lend some weight to the charge that Grant was an unimaginative bruiser who won, in the end, simply because he had overpowering numbers and used them remorselessly and without finesse.

So the Virginia campaign, which began when the Army of the Potomac crossed the Rapidan early in May, 1864, needs close examination.

One or two points need to be made clear at the beginning.

In the first place it is quite inaccurate to argue that no other Federal general ever enjoyed the over-all authority that was given to Grant when he became general-in-chief. McClellan had that authority, beginning in the fall of 1861 and running through the winter of 1862. Like Grant, he blocked out a comprehensive campaign covering all the important theaters of the war; the difference was that he could not make anything happen the way he wanted it to happen. He could not compel Halleck and Buell to work together, in the west. He could not make Buell drive into East Tennessee, although he repeatedly warned the man that his own strategy in Virginia depended on an aggressive advance by Buell's army. He could not even make his own army move according to his own timetable. If he was presently removed from over-all command of the Federal armies, the reason obviously was that he had not been able to exercise that over-all command effectively.

Halleck became general-in-chief early in the summer of 1862, and there is no question that President Lincoln hoped that he would be a vigorous commander. Halleck simply did not try to become one. The full authority Grant was finally given was

Halleck's, when Halleck first came to Washington; but Halleck refused to reach out, seize it, and exercise it, and in a remarkably short time he had reduced himself to a sort of high-level adviser, a paper-shuffler who neither laid down nor enforced a comprehensive strategy for the war as a whole. President Lincoln rendered his own verdict on the man not long after the battle of Fredericksburg, when General Burnside wanted to renew the offensive and his principal subordinates disagreed violently. The army was immobilized as a result, and Lincoln wrote Halleck suggesting that he, as general-in-chief, go down to Fredericksburg, examine the situation, and then either tell Burnside to go ahead, with full support from the top, or call the whole business off and devise something else. "In this difficulty, if you do not help me," Lincoln wrote to Halleck, "you fail me precisely in the point for which I sought your assistance." [8]

This hurt Halleck's feelings, so that he offered to resign, and in the War Department files Lincoln's original letter presently got an addition, in the President's handwriting: "Withdrawn, because considered harsh by General Halleck." As commanding general, Halleck simply refused to function, and the overriding authority that had been given to him withered on the vine because he was incapable of using it. The point to remember, however, is that the authority was there for him to use if he had had the force to exert it.

In addition, the authority which was at last given to Grant was not really as all-inclusive as it is usually supposed to have been, a fact which had a profound effect on the course of military operations.

Grant did not have the full control which he is assumed to have had. He was not, for instance, able to cancel General Nathaniel Banks's ill-advised and desperately unlucky offensive along the Red River—an eccentric thrust which was political rather than military in its conception, which would not have accomplished a great deal even if it had succeeded, and which used men, ships, and materiel that might have been applied elsewhere to much better advantage. Grant had no use for this movement, but not until Banks ran into outright disaster was he able to get it withdrawn.

More important, Grant was not able to select the commanders for two very important subsidiary movements in Virginia: movements which were well conceived and which, if they had been handled skillfully, would almost certainly have enabled Grant to win over Lee the kind of victory he had counted on winning.

One Union army was ordered to proceed up the Shenandoah Valley, depriving the Army of Northern Virginia of the bountiful supplies which it got from that area and, eventually, threatening Richmond from the west. Another army was ordered to advance toward Richmond along the south bank of the James River. The movements of these two armies were as much a part of Grant's Virginia campaign as the movements of the Army of the Potomac itself. If they had gone as scheduled—as they might very well have done if they had been efficiently led—the job which had to be done by the Army of the Potomac would have been ever so much easier. Taken all together, the triple-headed campaign would have been something the Confederacy probably could not have met.

But Grant was not able to get men of his own choice to command either of these subsidiary offensives.

The army which moved up the Shenandoah was put under General Franz Sigel, who was about as completely incompetent a commander as the Union army possessed. Sigel got his job solely because his name had, or was thought to have, political value with the large German-born population. The year 1864 was an election year, and Washington decided that it was necessary to give Sigel prominence. And Sigel's Shenandoah campaign collapsed almost before it had got started. Sigel was dismally routed at New Market, and his army instead of helping the operations of the Army of the Potomac became a source of weakness.

It was the same with the advance up the James. This advance was entrusted to General Ben Butler, of whom it must be said that he was probably Sigel's equal in military incompetence; and Butler most certainly would not have been in command if Grant had had anything to say about it. Butler had the strength to drive right to the outskirts of Richmond, and if he had done this Lee would have been compelled to retreat, or to make ruinously expensive detachments of force, just when the Army of the Potomac was pressing him most severely. As it worked out, however, Butler completely missed his opportunity, and before long permitted himself to be penned up in defensive works at Bermuda Hundred. Lee did not have to detach troops to oppose Butler; on the contrary, Lee was presently reinforced by some of the troops whom Butler should have been keeping busy.

In other words, Grant's Virginia campaign did not go as he had planned it partly because the two subsidiary moves which were essential to the whole design were commanded by inept soldiers who would never have been allowed within miles of the field of operations if Grant had had his way. No appraisal of what Grant did in Virginia is complete if the abysmal failure of these two offensives is not taken into account.

Grant's authority, in other words, was not really as unadulterated as is generally supposed. If the armies in the Shenandoah and along the James had been commanded by real soldiers —by such men, for instance, as John Sedgwick (whom Meade originally proposed for the Shenandoah command) and W. F. Smith—it is obvious that the job which had to be done by Meade's army would have been much easier and, presumably, would have gone much more smoothly. Grant was handicapped by Washington's interference here precisely as McClellan was handicapped when he launched his own offensive in the spring of 1862.

In any case, Grant as general-in-chief made his headquarters with the Army of the Potomac and took that Army across the Rapidan and into the Wilderness on May 4, 1864.

We badly need a detailed examination of the command arrangements which resulted. The army of course was under General George Meade's immediate command. (In the beginning, Burnside's corps, which accompanied the army, was not under Meade's control, but this was rectified before much time had passed.) Grant was present at all times, his own headquarters staff and apparatus being camped, usually, within a short distance of Meade's. The situation undoubtedly was difficult for both commanders: in effect, the army had two heads, Meade was under constant supervision, and on a good many occasions Grant and his staff issued battle orders direct to Meade's subordinates. Both Meade and Grant did their best to make this cumbrous system work, but it unquestionably led to many difficulties.

These difficulties, in addition, were complicated by the fact that the Army of the Potomac was clique-ridden. Its officer corps contained many men who still felt that only McClellan was a really good commander. They tended to resent the arrival of Grant, the westerner, to question his ability on the ground that the successes he had won in the west had been won against second-raters, and to express open skepticism about his ability to accomplish anything against a soldier of Lee's caliber. (One of the interesting things about the men who enjoyed important commands in the Army of the Potomac was that they seem to have had more respect for Lee than for any of their own superiors.) It seems possible at times to detect a certain sluggishness in army movements arising from this fact. At the very least it must be said that the dual command arrangement was a handicap.[9]

Whether for this reason or for some other, control of the army at corps and divisional level seems to have been defective. The kind of quick, decisive moment which characterized the movements of Grant's army in the Vicksburg campaign, for example, was not in evidence. Cold Harbor was very poorly managed, and the whole attempt to seize Petersburg following the crossing of the James was hopelessly bungled; it is hardly too much to say that during the two or three crucial days in which that key point should have been occupied by Union forces the army as an army was hardly commanded at all. (Indeed, Meade himself said virtually as much, almost in so many words. On June 18, when he had his last chance to drive into Petersburg before Lee's army arrived, he found it utterly impossible to get a co-ordinated advance, and at last he burst out with the revealing telegram to his subordinates: "I find it useless to appoint an hour to effect co-operation . . . what additional orders to attack you require I cannot imagine. . . . Finding it impossible to effect co-operation by appointing an hour for attack, I have sent an order to each corps commander to attack at all hazards, and without reference to each other." [10]) The attack failed, naturally enough, and the Confederates held Petersburg for nine more months. It might be noted, in this connection, that the soldiers in the Army of the Potomac fought well enough here; the war weariness which is supposed to have resulted from Cold Harbor, and from the wearing campaign which had preceded it, had not yet set in. It was the army commander's failure to control the battle that was the trouble here.

The army commander, to repeat, was Meade: but Grant was the general-in-chief, he was with the army at the time, and as the man who would have gained the credit if a great victory had been won he can probably be given blame for the failure. It is hard to escape the conclusion that it was the dual command arrangement that was largely at fault . . . hard, also, to avoid the feeling that if a Sheridan or a Thomas had been in Meade's place during those first few days at Petersburg the story would have been different.

However all of that may have been, one more complaint about Grant's generalship in the Virginia campaign must be examined: the charge that he had too much faith in the virtues of a head-on offensive and failed to recognize the immense preponderance of the defensive in frontal assaults like the ones at Spotsylvania and Cold Harbor.

It is undoubtedly true that Grant underestimated the defensive strength of good troops, well entrenched, using rifled muskets. He shared this failing with most of the other Civil War generals, including Lee himself. Weapons used in the Civil War, even though they look extremely primitive today, were in fact much more modern than anything warfare had seen before. A revolution in tactics was taking place, and it took the generals a long time to realize it. One is tempted to speculate that the success of Thomas' great assault at Chattanooga, where a massed army corps captured the Missionary Ridge position which should have been completely invulnerable to any frontal attack, may have stuck too long in the back of Grant's mind. Whatever the reason, it must be said that it took Grant a long time to see that the all-along-the-line attack after the old manner was out of date. A great many men died because of this.[11]

Summing up the criticisms of the Virginia campaign of 1864, then, one must say: (1) that the subsidiary campaigns which should have insured the success of the advance of the Army of the Potomac failed miserably because Grant was unable to control the appointment of the men who led them; (2) that the command arrangement which grew out of his insistence on accompanying Meade's army was most defective and probably was at least partly responsible for a number of costly setbacks; and (3) that Grant himself showed too much fondness for old-fashioned offensive combat when the conditions under which that kind of combat could have succeeded had disappeared.

Against these criticisms, balance Grant's achievements. They are more solid than is apparent at first glance.

First of all, and perhaps most important of all, Grant was the one Federal general, from first to last, who kept the initiative in the Virginia theater.

Each one of his predecessors had moved South in a great "Forward to Richmond" campaign, and each one of them had found before long that he had lost the ball and was on the defensive; instead of forcing Lee to keep step with him, the Federal general was always trying to keep step with Lee, usually without great success. McClellan, Pope, Burnside, Hooker, even Meade—each one went south to defeat a strongly outnumbered opponent and before long found either that he was in full retreat or that he was fighting desperately for survival. Here was the fact that had given the generals in the Army of the Potomac such vast respect for Lee's military ability. No matter how a campaign began, it usually ended with Lee calling the shots.

The second achievement grows out of the first.

By keeping the initiative, Grant compelled Lee to fight the kind of war which Lee could not win. Lee's conduct of the campaign which began in the Wilderness and ended at last in front of Petersburg was masterly, enormously costly in Northern lives, almost ruinous to home-front morale—the profound wave of war weariness which swept the North in the summer of 1864 came largely because the Virginia campaign was so dreadfully expensive and seemed to be accomplishing so little—but it did end with Lee locked up in a fortress where effective offensive movements were impossible for him. Not long after the Wilderness campaign began, Lee remarked that if he were ever forced back into the Richmond lines and compelled to stand on the defensive there the end would be only a matter of time.[12] He was, in spite of his best efforts, forced back into those lines; in spite of his magnificent tactical successes, the process took only a little more than six weeks; and after that it was, as Lee himself had predicted, just a question of time.

The campaign did, to be sure, reduce the fighting capacity of the valiant Army of the Potomac to a low level. Such excellent combat units as Hancock's II Corps, for example, late in the summer became almost impotent; at Reams Station this corps was routed by a Confederate counterattack which the same corps would have beaten off with ease six months earlier. But this grim process of attrition worked both ways. The Army of Northern Virginia was worn down also, so that it likewise became unable to do things which in earlier years it would have done smoothly. The Federal cause could endure this attrition and the Southern cause could not.

Yet it was not actually just a campaign of attrition. The significant thing is that Lee was deprived of the opportunity to maneuver, to seize the openings created by his opponent's mistakes, to make full use of the dazzling ability to combine swift movements and hard blows which had served him so well in former campaigns. Against Grant, Lee was not able to do the things he had done before. He had to fight the sort of fight he could not win.

Finally, even though Grant's original hope was to bring Lee to battle in the open and destroy his army, he was really conducting an immense holding operation, and what happened in Virginia means nothing unless it is examined in the light of what was happening elsewhere. Sherman was advancing in and through Georgia. Unless the Confederacy could intervene against him, Sherman would eventually provide the winning maneuver. Grant held Lee down so effectively that intervention against Sherman became impossible; holding Lee, Grant insured Sherman's victory. When Sherman won, the war was won. Lee, to be sure, held out to the bitter end, but the end came because the Confederacy behind Lee had shrunk to a helpless fragment.

It gets back, in other words, to the grand strategy, the concept of the war as a whole in which the movements of all of the Federal armies were interrelated. What Grant did in Virginia enabled the grand strategy to work. Viewed in that light, the Virginia campaign was a success: costly, agonizing, all but unendurably grueling in its demands on soldiers and on the people back home, but still a success.

Grant, in short, was able to use the immense advantage in numbers, in military resources, and in money which the Federal side possessed from the start. Those advantages had always been there, and what the Northern war effort had always needed was a soldier who, assuming the top command, would see to it that they were applied steadily, remorselessly and without a break, all across the board. The complaint that Grant succeeded only because he had superior numbers is pointless. The superior numbers were part of the equation all along. It was Grant who took advantage of them and used them to apply a pressure which the weaker side could not possibly stand.

This was a most substantial achievement. Achieving it, Grant merits very high ranking as a soldier. He used the means at hand to discharge the obligation which had been put upon him. The war was won thereby, and it is not easy to see how it would have been won without Grant.

NOTES

1. Lee to Governor John Letcher, December 26, 1861, *Southern Historical Society Papers,* I (1876), 462.

2. *War of the Rebellion: A Compilation of the Official Records of the Union and Confederate Armies* (Washington, 1880–1901), Series I, Vol. XVI, part 1, p. 51. Cited hereafter as *Official Records;* all references are to Series I.

3. Speech of John A. Rawlins, in the *Proceedings of the Society of the Army of the Tennessee* (Cincinnati, 1866).

4. *Personal Memoirs of U. S. Grant* (New York, 1885), I, 273–74; A. L. Conger, *The Rise of U. S. Grant* (New York, 1931), pp. 99–101.

5. John W. Emerson, "Grant's Life in the West," *Midland Monthly Magazine,* VI (1896).

6. Edward A. Pollard, *The Lost Cause* (New York, 1866), p. 202.

7. Details regarding the delays in the Union advance preceding Shiloh are summarized in this writer's *Grant Moves South* (Boston, 1960), pp. 210–15.

8. *Official Records,* XXI, 940, 944–45, 953–54.

9. Peter S. Michie, *The Life and Letters of Emory Upton* (New York, 1885), pp. 108–09; James H. Wilson, *Under the Old Flag* (New York, 1912), I, 400.

10. *Official Records,* XL, 167, 179, 205.

11. There is an excellent discussion of the effect on Civil War tactics of improved firepower in J. F. C. Fuller, *The Generalship of Ulysses S. Grant* (London, 1929).

12. Douglas Southall Freeman, *R. E. Lee* (New York, 1934–35), III, 398.

The Generalship of Robert E. Lee

by CHARLES P. ROLAND

MACHIAVELLI wrote that victory is the final test of skill in war. "If a general wins a battle," he said, "it cancels all other errors and miscarriages." Conversely, one may infer, if a general loses a battle, it cancels all other brilliance and daring. Experience in two world wars, followed by a growing insecurity in the modern age, heightens the American sense of nationalism today. Supreme excellence in all things (whether economic, intellectual, or military) must come of our peculiar political and social institutions, Americans are accustomed to believe. Rudely upset in the field of science by Sputnik, Gagarin, and Titov, this happy theme yet pervades much of the literature of American history, and especially many recent treatises on the Civil War. Provincialism and conservatism restricted the Confederate military mind, say our nationalistic scholars, and assured victory to the Union. Here are the major problems in expounding the talents of Robert E. Lee: for he fought against the Union; and he is the only American general who has ever lost a war.

Fortunately, insofar as Lee's reputation is concerned, history sometimes flouts the inference from Machiavelli's rule: occasionally a great genius in war—a Hannibal, a Charles XII, or a Napoleon—falls in defeat. These exceptions to such a law of success and failure in war demonstrate that generalship alone does not always prevail, however good it may be. Victory requires that one side overmatch the opposite in the sum of its generalship plus all other capabilities for waging war. Hence, judged fairly, a general's record must be weighed against the resources at his command.

Lee and the Confederacy opposed awesome superiority in the means of making war. "All else equal," said Clausewitz, "numbers will determine victory in combat. . . . In ordinary cases an important superiority of numbers, but which need not be over two to one, will be sufficient to ensure victory, however disadvantageous other circumstances may be." Early in the war Southern troops were outnumbered 2 to 1; before war's end they were outnumbered 3 to 1.[1] In industrial strength, the decisive weapon of modern war, the Confederacy was hopelessly overmatched: in 1860, for example, the North produced 20 times as much pig iron as did the South, and 24 times as many locomotive engines. At like disadvantage today, the United States would be pitted against an adversary manufacturing annually one billion tons of steel, along with comparable quantities of automotive and other industrial wares. The United States census-taker in 1865 wrote with candor that the Confederacy fell for want of material resources, and not for lack of will, skill, or courage. Forge and lathe, plow and reaper, rail and piston: all weighed in the balance against Lee and his associates.[2]

Since the South must be invaded and conquered before Federal authority could reassert itself, the Confederacy held the strategic advantage of interior, or shorter, lines of communication. Theoretically, she was able more rapidly to concentrate troops upon points of decision than could the Union. Actually, this was seldom true. Possessing less than half the railway mileage that the North had, and virtually no facilities for manufacturing or repairing locomotives and rolling stock, the Confederacy was unable to profit significantly from interior lines. Early in the war she lost the railroads of western and central Tennessee, including a long stretch of the vital Memphis and Charleston track. Command of these roads and of the upper Mississippi River and the lower Tennessee River gave to the Union forces the interior lines of communication within the broad western theater of the Confederacy. Unable to control the seas, the Confederacy fought with flank and rear continuously threatened with invasion.

Lee and the Confederate government had also to contend with the powerful influence of localism within the Confederacy. Asserting the rights of state sovereignty, many Southern governors withheld large numbers of men from the Confederate armies, and demanded protection of all territory within their states. The institution of slavery aggravated this tendency; even the temporary appearance of Northern troops in any part of the South so disrupted the labor force and the economy that they could never be returned to normal. Hence, Confederate authorities were obliged to scatter many thousands of troops at scores of points having little strategic importance, if any.

Though Lee was not responsible for the general strategy of the defensive adopted by Jefferson Davis early in the war, Lee tacitly indorsed it. Some Confederate leaders urged a prompt invasion of the North; they called for a lightning stroke against the people of the Union, before her vast resources could be mobilized. Certain historians today support this strategy by pointing out that in a prolonged war of attrition the South was foredoomed to defeat.

Critics speak with authority in disparaging Confederate strategy; they speak with uncertain voices in saying what it ought to have been. Offensive war against the North would seem to have been futile. Four years were required for the immensely more powerful Union to conquer the Confederacy; that the South could have conquered the North is inconceivable. Through the defensive, the South could conserve her lesser strength and exact of the North a heavier toll in blood and treasure. Doubtless unwittingly, Southern leaders followed Clausewitz's dictum, "Defense is the stronger form of war." Even that implacable critic of Confederate leadership, General J. F. C. Fuller, acknowledges that the defensive was the only sound policy for the South.[3]

Exigencies of Southern politics, society, and logistics caused Davis to adopt, and Lee to second, a strategy of territorial defense. Accordingly, the Confederacy was split into departments (or theaters), each with its own army, and each to be defended against invasion, with no territory to be yielded voluntarily to the enemy. Such a design fell short of the military rule, "Unity of plan, concentration of force." Lee was aware that this strategy failed to achieve maximum concentration of force; that it thus violated the fundamental principle of war as set forth by the military theorist Henri Jomini, whom Lee is nowadays accused of following slavishly. But in fashioning this plan, Confederate leaders anticipated a principle of modern warfare not then generally recognized; they sought to provide what Cyril Falls describes as ". . . that vital factor of the most recent times, the defence of the home base and civil population." [4]

In condemning this failure to concentrate, General Fuller says that the Confederacy ought to have yielded temporarily the state of Virginia and other areas of the upper South in order to mass her forces at the key rail center Chattanooga. By harassing Union communications and drawing Union armies away from base, he opines, the Confederacy may then have struck a decisive blow with her entire *grande armée*. As military science in the narrow sense, this may be sound, though it tempts the speculation that such an initial Confederate concentration would merely have caused a like Union concentration, but in far greater strength. "Concentration *a priori* and without regard to enemy dispositions invites disaster," writes General de Gaulle in a perceptive comment on French operations in World War I. As strategy in the highest sense, strategy that blends military science with political science, social psychology, and economics, General Fuller's plan is folly. Abandonment of the upper South to the Shermans and Sheridans of the Northern army would have undone the Confederacy without a battle. "There is nothing in [Lee's] generalship," says Sir Frederic

Maurice, "which is more striking than the manner in which he grasped the problems of the Confederacy and . . . adapted his strategy both to the cause for which the South was fighting and to the major political conditions of the time." Considering the circumstances of Southern life, territorial defense was probably the only strategy open to the leaders of the Confederacy.[5]

As adviser to President Davis early in the war, Lee did not decide strategy; he was in no sense general-in-chief of Confederate armies. "Broadly speaking," says biographer Douglas Southall Freeman, "Davis entrusted to [Lee] the minor, vexatious matters of detail and the counselling of commanders in charge of the smaller armies. On the larger strategic issues the President usually consulted with him and was often guided by his advice, but in no single instance was Lee given a free hand to initiate and direct to full completion any plan of magnitude." [6]

Restricted as he was by the character of his assignment, Lee nevertheless at this time showed deep insight into the nature of the war, and urged certain measures that would greatly strengthen the South for the struggle ahead. In the early days after Fort Sumter, when many people of the South still predicted that there would be no war, and that, if it should come, it would be quickly won by Southern arms, Lee said that war was inevitable, and that it would be long and bloody. In the fall, 1861, when many thought that England was about to enter the war against the North because of the *Trent* affair, Lee warned against such hope. "We must make up our minds to fight our battles and win independence alone," he wrote prophetically. "No one will help us." [7]

When in Februrary, 1862, Forts Henry and Donelson fell, and the Confederate Army in the west was threatened with destruction, Lee wisely advised stripping the Gulf Coast of troops in order to reinforce Albert Sidney Johnston and Beauregard at Corinth, Mississippi. To Johnston, Lee gave sound strategic counsel: concentrate, said Lee, and strike the enemy at your front before the two wings of his army can be joined. The battle of Shiloh, fought according to this plan, came within an inch of destroying the Union army there: neither side would again come so close to a total victory until exhaustion had overtaken the Confederacy at war's end.[8]

Lee's support of conscription to muster the manpower of the South indicated advanced military thinking and willingness to break with American precedent. As early as December, 1861, Lee recommended state conscription by the government of Virginia: after Confederate losses at Shiloh and New Orleans the following spring, Lee's indorsement of Confederate conscription helped to secure passage of the act by the Southern Congress. Lee's ideas on conscription offer proof of how far beyond Jomini he had gone during the first year of the Civil War. Jomini considered war an affair to be settled by professional armies; he refused to contemplate a people's war, and wrote, "[It] would be so terrible that, for the sake of humanity, we ought never to see it." Lee said, "Since the whole duty of the nation [will] be war until independence [is] secured, the whole nation should for a time be converted into an army, the producers to feed and the soldiers to fight." Not until the outbreak of World War I would the governments of the world grasp fully this principle of total mobilization laid down by Lee almost threescore years before.[9]

In the spring, 1862, as McClellan's powerful army moved to the Virginia Peninsula and threatened Richmond at close quarters, Davis leaned heavily upon Lee for support. Lee's talent as a strategist now began to emerge in his daring shift of Confederate troops to oppose McClellan's advance. But Lee saw the futility of meeting the Federal concentration with like concentration; he realized that the smaller Southern force must ultimately be overwhelmed if this were done. Instead, Lee adopted the more resourceful technique of weakening McClellan's army by threatening a blow at the North. "As to dividing the enemy's strength," wrote Machiavelli, "there can be no better way . . . than by making incursions into their country. . . ." From relatively unexposed points in the Carolinas and Georgia, Lee drew reinforcements piecemeal for the Confederate army on the Peninsula: meantime, Lee urged General Jackson in the Shenandoah Valley to strike the enemy there in order to divert Northern troops from McClellan. This was the genesis of Lee's later strategy for the entire Confederacy.[10]

On May 31, 1862, Confederate General Joseph E. Johnston fell wounded in the fighting on the Peninsula, and Davis named Lee to command the Army of Northern Virginia. Lee's mission was to defend Virginia, and especially the Confederate capital, Richmond. He opposed the strongest of Union concentrations, which outnumbered his own force by 2 to 1. For three years Lee would fulfill his mission against the heaviest odds ever faced by an American commander.

The wisdom of defending Richmond, to the relative neglect of other points in the South, has been seriously questioned. Defense of the capital to the bitter end cannot be justified; but there was reason for holding it as long as possible without sacrificing the army. Even if Richmond had possessed no intrinsic military value, as the capital it had great symbolic value. One may lightly disparage both Davis and Lincoln for waging long and bitter campaigns for the capture or protection of idle cities; yet both men sensed the psychological importance of being able to retain the seat of government. Winston Churchill recognized this principle when late in World War II he urged that Berlin was still an objective of great strategic importance; that nothing else would blight German morale so much as would the fall of Berlin. Moreover, Richmond was by no means an idle city: she contained the great parent-arsenal of the South, the Tredegar Works, besides many other armories and factories. To the Confederacy, Richmond was Washington and Pittsburgh in one. Aside from symbolic and material values, northern Virginia possessed great strategic value for the Confederacy. It was a dagger pointed toward the heart of the enemy, a potential base for strikes against the Northern capital and the great northeastern centers of population, industry, and communication. A powerful, mobile Southern army in northern Virginia was the most effective instrument of the Confederacy for paralyzing the mind of President Lincoln and the will of the Northern people.

Lee preferred this command to all others, since it would keep him in his beloved Virginia. Though Davis made the decision to defend Richmond, Lee unquestionably approved of it.

Once in command, Lee instantly did what he would always do as long as he had the strength for it; he seized the initiative in the campaign. His strategy for weakening McClellan's force had already borne fruit; Jackson's spectacular demonstration in the Valley (April 30–June 9) caused President Lincoln to divert McDowell's corps there. Ordering Jackson to Richmond by rail, Lee now attempted a concerted blow against McClellan. Faulty staff work and the derelictions of subordinates may have cost Lee a decisive victory. Nevertheless, in a series of fierce engagements (June 26–July 2) Lee persuaded McClellan to abandon the drive for Richmond.[11]

Blunting of McClellan's thrust enabled Lee to open what Davis called an offensive-defensive against the Union armies in Virginia. From the beginning, Lee knew that his army could not withstand a siege by the vastly stronger Northern numbers opposing it. Lee must keep the enemy forces divided; he could not afford for them to concentrate upon him. In order to prevent such concentration, he must constantly maneuver and confound his opponents with threats against Washington and with lightning blows against exposed fractions of their strength. Second Manassas was a brilliant demonstration of this technique.

In mid-July Lee learned that Federal troops were concentrating under General John Pope on the Rapidan River in northern Virginia. Lee had to decide quickly whether the next Union main effort was to be from the north or from the Peninsula. Sensing that it would be made by Pope, Lee started Jackson's corps north by rail; when on August 13 Lee learned that the Union force on the James was being reduced, he reasoned that these troops were being sent to Pope. Lee then rushed the remainder of his army up to strike Pope before McClellan's reinforcements could reach him. By dividing the Confederate army and sending Jackson around Pope's flank to threaten communications with Washington, Lee unsettled his adversary and forced him out of position. Reuniting Longstreet and Jackson on the battlefield, Lee then defeated Pope (August 29–30, 1862) and drove him back to the Washington earthworks.

Lee's decision to move his army from the James to the Rapidan showed seeming uncanny ability to anticipate the enemy; it has been called a supreme example of the manner in which judgment and boldness must supplement available information in shaping strategy. Lee's shift of force was a lesson in the use of interior lines of communication and the strategic employment of railroads. Dividing the Confederate army in the face of superior numbers violated the rules of warfare; Jomini warned against it; Lee was criticized for doing it. But Clausewitz says, "What genius does must be the best of all rules, and theory cannot do better than to show how and why it is so." Lee himself gave the explanation. "The disparity . . . between the contending forces rendered the risks unavoidable," he said.[12]

With the Federal army reeling under defeat, and his own troops flushed with victory, Lee now determined to carry the war to the enemy. He proposed to invade Maryland and Pennsylvania. Invasion of the North would extend Lee's war of maneuver; it would find provisions for his troops; and it would free Virginia of molestation during the harvest. A successful campaign across the Potomac might do much more than this;

it might add Maryland to the Confederacy; it might sever communications between northeast and northwest; it might place the great cities of the east at Lee's command; and it might bring foreign recognition. It might even end the war, thought Lee; and he proposed that Davis offer peace with honor to the North at this time.

In early September Lee crossed the Potomac. Segments of his army were spread wide to cut the railroads and isolate McClellan from reinforcements. Here the fates deserted Lee. His appeal to the people of Maryland fell on deaf ears. Far worse, McClellan moved against him with disconcerting assurance. One of the traits of a great general is his insight into the character of the opposing general: the ability, as Colonel G. F. R. Henderson phrases it, "to penetrate the adversary's brain." In this faculty, Lee has had few peers. On the eve of marching into Maryland, he said, "McClellan's army will not be prepared for offensive operations—or he will not think it so—for three or four weeks. Before that time I hope to be on the Susquehanna." Ordinarily, Lee would have been right about McClellan; but something extraordinary happened on this occasion. Providentially supplied with a copy of Lee's plan of campaign, found wrapped around three cigars on the ground, McClellan struck Lee's divided army and came near destroying it at Sharpsburg on September 16–17. Lee held McClellan off and won tactical victory; but Lee was obliged to return to Virginia and abandon the campaign.[13]

In striking at the North and her capital, say some scholars today, Lee again was simply obeying the stale rules of warfare as set forth by Jomini, or by his chief American disciple, Professor Dennis Hart Mahan of West Point. Actually, Lee was using a strategy as old as war itself; and as modern, too. "If the defender has gained an important advantage," says Clausewitz, "then the defensive form has done its part, and under the protection of this success he must give back the blow. . . . Common sense points out that iron should be struck while it is hot. . . . A swift and vigorous assumption of the offensive—the flashing sword of vengeance—is the most brilliant point in the defensive." This principle was alike sound for Scipio Africanus, or Frederick the Great, or George Catlett Marshall. It was also sound for Lee.[14]

In retrospect, the grander aims of Lee's campaigns into the North seem visionary. Probably England and France would have remained neutral even if Lee had won a victory on Northern soil; that the Lincoln administration would have accepted a peace offer is unlikely. But Lee did not have the advantage of hindsight. The true goal in war, says Clausewitz, is to subject the enemy to one's will. Often this can be done only through destroying the enemy's armed forces. But this is not the sole method for accomplishing the object of war, continues Clausewitz: moreover, when one lacks the resources to destroy the enemy's armed forces, he must resort to other means; he must then attempt to destroy the enemy's will through measures short of the destruction of his military power. Among such, says the German theorist, are the seizure of the enemy's capital, or the inflicting of casualties beyond the enemy's expectations. Here was just Lee's situation.[15]

Lee knew that the South could not possibly destroy the war strength of the North, however successful in battle the South might be; that, ironically, Southern victories in the field weakened the South in men and material resources relatively more than they weakened the North. Shortly after his greatest triumph (Chancellorsville), Lee wrote to Davis, "We should not . . . conceal from ourselves that our resources in men are constantly diminishing, and the disproportion in this respect between us and our enemies . . . is steadily augmenting."[16] Only by paralyzing the Northern will to victory could the South hope to achieve her war aims. Lee was aware that Washington had no intrinsic military value. But he knew also that

President Lincoln and the Northern people had invested the city with great symbolic value; and he knew that defeat at home shakes a population more than defeat in a distant land. He believed that a successful invasion of the North by a victorious Confederate army was most likely to exalt his own people and to blight the morale of the enemy. Considered in this light, his decisions to invade the North are reasonable.

In Virginia again after the fruitless Maryland campaign, Lee dispersed his army, recruited his strength, and braced for another Federal assault. It came in mid-December against the impregnable heights of Fredericksburg. Reconcentrating quickly, Lee met the attack pointblank. Bloodily repulsed, the Northern army fell back across the Rapidan to await a new commander and a new occasion.

Spring of 1863 found the lines of the Confederacy holding fast in the east but deeply pierced in the west. New Orleans was lost; Grant pressed upon Vicksburg; and Rosecrans was lodged in central Tennessee, threatening Chattanooga. Davis and his counselors sought desperately for a strategy that would restore the balance in the west. Many plans were offered. Most of them called for a shift of troops from relatively secure points elsewhere to the faltering armies of the west in the hope of concentrating sufficient strength there to win decisively over Grant or Rosecrans, or both. In early March, Lee told Davis that for some time he had hoped that the situation in Virginia would enable him to detach an entire corps of his army to the support of the west. Secretary of War Seddon strongly urged this move; and Generals Longstreet and Beauregard set forth variations of it. But the strength and activity of the Army of the Potomac, now commanded by General Joseph Hooker, prevented such an operation at this time, thought Lee. A month later, as affairs in the west grew worse, Secretary of War Seddon called upon Lee to consider sending one division there. Seddon's request for Lee's views on this measure caused Lee to formulate a general strategy for meeting the crisis.

In principle, the strategy now expounded by Lee was not new to him; rather, it was an elaboration of his ingrained philosophy of war, as adapted to the peculiar needs of the Confederacy. Lee agreed with Davis and Seddon that the situation required boldness; that the Confederate armies in the west ought at once to take the initiative. Let Joseph E. Johnston concentrate and attack Grant in Mississippi, recommended Lee; let Bragg strike into Kentucky and threaten Ohio. But Lee cautioned against weakening the Army of Northern Virginia; Hooker would not stand idle, predicted Lee, but soon would strike a powerful blow against Virginia. An advocate of the maximum concentration of force against isolated segments of the enemy, Lee nevertheless felt that, in this instance, the distances were too great and the transport facilities of the South too feeble to justify such a move. The Confederacy could not match the Union in shifting troops from one department to another, he said; to rely on that method might render Confederate reserves always too late.

To prevent the North from transferring troops in order to concentrate at a given point, Lee said that all Southern commanders ought to take the offensive upon any weakening of the enemy on their fronts. Let Confederate armies in the major departments be reinforced from the less exposed departments of the deep South, he advised—from the vicinity of Charleston, Savannah, Mobile, and Vicksburg. Lee's curious listing of Vicksburg came of an erroneous notion that Federal operations there would soon have to quit because of the pestilential Mississippi summer. Apparently Davis, whose home was but a few miles from Vicksburg, never disabused Lee of this idea.

Lee's prime recommendation was that he again strike at the North with his own army. "The readiest method of relieving pressure upon General Joseph E. Johnston," said Lee, "is for the [Army of Northern Virginia] to cross into Maryland. . . . Greater relief would in this way be afforded to the armies in middle Tennessee." To penetrate the enemy's vitals, or if this were impossible, to threaten them with Clausewitz's "flashing sword of vengeance"—this was the key to Lee's strategy.

True to Lee's prediction, in late April Hooker advanced in Virginia. Again Lee seized the initiative with great audacity. Splitting the Confederate force, Lee occupied the bulk of Hooker's powerful army with slightly above one-third of his own; at the same time Lee sent the remainder of his troops under the indomitable Jackson to fall upon Hooker's vulnerable flank and rear. Lee's victory at Chancellorsville (May 2–3), says Colonel Henderson, was one of the supreme instances in history of a great general's ability to outwit his adversary and direct the attack where it is least expected. The Army of the Potomac once more fell back across the Rapidan; Confederate leaders again took inventory of strategic resources.[17]

Anxious over the security of Vicksburg, Secretary of War Seddon again proposed the shift of troops from Lee's army to support Pemberton on the Mississippi. If necessary, replied Lee, order Pickett's division to the west. But Lee warned anew that the great distance required by the move, plus the uncertainty of employment of Pickett's troops in Mississippi, made the venture inadvisable. Weakening of the Army of Northern Virginia, he felt, might force it to retire into the Richmond defenses, where it would cease to be a formidable instrument of Confederate strategy. Davis and his cabinet met with Lee on May 16 and, with Postmaster General Reagan possibly dissenting, approved Lee's plan to invade the North again. This meant that Confederate armies in the west must fend for themselves.

Already a part of Lee's army was on the move toward Pennsylvania. As he put his troops in motion, Lee searched the Confederacy for reinforcements and pondered other measures that would strengthen his blow. Earlier he had called upon Davis to bring idle troops from the Carolinas, Georgia, and Florida to the Army of Northern Virginia; if necessary, Lee had advised, strip the coastal garrisons except for enough men to operate the water batteries. He now repeated this plea and added another recommendation. Let General Beauregard come with these reserves to northern Virginia, Lee said, and there create a diversion in favor of the advance into Pennsylvania. Anxiety of the Northern government over the safety of Washington would cause a large force to be left for protection of the capital, Lee believed. Beauregard ought to command the diversionary column in person, said Lee. "His presence would give magnitude to even a small demonstration and tend greatly to perplex and confound the enemy." A mere "army in effigy" under Beauregard would have good effect, thought Lee, if no more troops than this were available.

Thinking the North shaken by Chancellorsville and the threat of Confederate invasion, Lee again advised a Southern peace overture. The South ought not to demand peace unconditionally, he said; rather, she ought to encourage the peace party of the North to believe that the Union could be restored by negotiation. "Should the belief that peace will bring back the Union become general, the war would no longer be supported. . . ." he observed. Once hostilities ended, he believed that they would not be resumed, and that Southern independence would thus be achieved.

Gettysburg was Lee's debacle. Again fortune turned upon him; at Brandy Station, on the eve of the march into Pennsylvania, Federal cavalry seized Confederate correspondence indicating a northward move by Lee. Davis made no effort to bring up reinforcements or to create the army in effigy requested by Lee. Exceeding Lee's orders, Jeb Stuart rode amiss and deprived Lee of his "eyes," the cavalry, so that he groped his way into Pennsylvania without knowing the whereabouts of the

Union army. General Ewell, recently elevated to corps commander as a result of Jackson's death, proved unequal to his responsibilities and failed to seize the key position, Cemetery Hill, early in the battle, when it probably could have been taken. Longstreet sulked and was sluggish in attacking Cemetery Ridge on the second day. Lee erred gravely in ordering the frontal assault against Cemetery Ridge on the third day, when it was impregnably held. After three days of carnage, Lee retreated into Virginia. The tide of the Confederacy was spent.[18]

That in the Gettysburg campaign Lee was below his best goes without saying. His more severe critics see in the Gettysburg decision a narrow provincialism that blinded Lee to the war as a whole. In contrast to Lee's strategy, which the critics say was primarily a defense of Virginia, they see in the plan urged by Seddon, Longstreet, and Beauregard a truly comprehensive Confederate military design. It would have been a Jominian stroke on the grand scale, they say, taking advantage of the Confederacy's interior lines of communication, and concentrating a maximum of Confederate strength for the destruction of Rosecrans' isolated army in Tennessee. Thus Lee becomes the culprit who squandered the Confederacy's one opportunity to win the war.[19]

This criticism is highly problematical. It rests upon the present knowledge that Lee's plan was tried, at least in part, and that it failed. The critics assume what cannot be known: that western concentration was more likely to succeed than was Lee's eastern offensive. Exponents of western concentration do not take into account the logistical weaknesses of the South, which Lee felt made the western venture impractical. After the war, Confederate General E. P. Alexander had a vision of a powerful Confederate "army on wheels" using the interior lines of the South to shuttle rapidly back and forth between engagements east and west. Alas for the Confederacy, this could be but a vision. Southern troops could, of course, move somewhat more quickly from Virginia to Tennessee than could Northern troops, who had more than twice as far to go. But continued shifting of a large army to and fro across the South, as Alexander contemplated, was roughly the equivalent in time and effort of a like movement across Siberia today. Lee well knew the military significance of railroads; many of his campaigns had been skillful demonstrations in the strategic and logistical use of them. But he accurately sensed that Northern railroad superiority largely nullified the Confederacy's theoretical advantage of interior lines on a grand scale. General Alexander's plan was beyond the capacity of Southern transport and industry; it probably would have exhausted the Confederacy without a battle.[20]

Supporters of the western plan exaggerate the probability of decisive victory over Rosecrans and minimize the effect of weakening Lee's army as a major strategic weapon of the Confederacy. To achieve the purpose of the western effort, Confederate forces there had to do more than win a battle; they must win so prodigiously as to cause the North to quit the war. That a western Confederate victory of any degree would have done this is questionable. Complete defeat or capture of Rosecrans' army would not have destroyed the war capacity of the Union; her major striking force was elsewhere. One may further question that a total victory over Rosecrans was likely, even granting the maximum Confederate concentration. Walter Millis has pointed out that the advent of railroad, steamboat, and telegraph ended the great battlefield decisions of finality.[21] No such victory was won by either side in the Civil War, regardless of numerical advantage, until the last stages of weakness and demoralization had come upon the Confederacy. If the South could, in any event, have won a western victory of such magnitude as to end the war, she could have done it probably only through three conditions: Rosecrans must obligingly remain exposed to destruction until the Confederacy could mass her strength against him; Hooker with the most powerful of Union armies must sit idle in the east all the while; and the western Confederate force, hastily assembled from all over the South, must operate free of the very kind of miscarriage that plagued Lee's veteran army—the varsity team—in its Pennsylvania offensive. That any of these circumstances would have prevailed seems doubtful; that all of them would have prevailed seems incredible.

Nevertheless, everything ought to have been hazarded for the west, it is said; the war was lost in the west. This would appear to be only half truth; it obscures that the war was lost in east and west, and through a long process of exhaustion. The west was not intrinsically more valuable to the Confederacy than was the east; once the east was taken, the west would surely fall. The Confederacy could not live without both east and west.

Close examination of Lee's strategy refutes the accusation that it was merely a defense of Virginia. It was a comprehensive strategy for the Confederacy, however faulty it may have been. Interestingly, it was in some ways quite like Grant's later strategy for the Union: it employed Lee's seemingly invincible army, greatly strengthened, as the major Confederate striking force; and it called for simultaneous offensives by all major Confederate armies to prevent Northern concentration upon any one of them. It was designed, in part, to nullify the Northern advantages in transportation that enabled her to shift troops swiftly from one department to another. Lee's plan for an army in effigy under Beauregard was a superbly ingenious stratagem that might well have upset a nervous foe. It anticipated by almost a century General Patton's mock invasion of the Pas de Calais coast in World War II, which helped to deceive the German high command and to free the Normandy beachheads from heavy counterattack for many precious days.[22] Lee's request was worthy of strenuous effort to fulfill it.

Finally, Lee's plan would have cured the major ill in the deployment of Southern manpower; it would have drawn strategic reserves from the minor departments of the Confederacy to the main effort. Throughout most of the war, excessive numbers of Confederate troops were scattered at relatively idle stations about the South. In early 1863, total Confederate armies were outnumbered 2 to 1: but the major Confederate armies at this time faced odds of 2.5 to 1, while Confederate garrisons along the Atlantic Coast actually outnumbered the opposing Union armies. In the departments of the Carolinas, Georgia, and Florida, 45,000 Confederates opposed 27,000 Federals. From these troops, and others at various places in Virginia, Lee could have added an entire corps to his army, with enough left over to guard the coast and form Beauregard's army in effigy as well.[23]

In a word, Lee proposed to apply to the entire Confederacy the strategy that he had successfully employed within his own department. With offensives throughout the South he would keep the total enemy force divided; with diversions in northern Virginia he would confound and divide the local enemy force; then, with the strongest, the most skillful, and the most cohesive army of the Confederacy, he would direct his main effort against the vital center of the North.

Lee asked for a diversionary force too late for Davis to create it, under the circumstances, even if he had attempted it. Lee proposed this ruse on June 23, only a week before Gettysburg. By now many of the troops from the Atlantic Coast had been sent, without Lee's certain knowledge, to Mississippi, where they would accomplish nothing. This suggests a further thought in weighing Lee's role in the Gettysburg decision. Lee was not general-in-chief of Confederate armies; he was still merely commander of the Army of Northern Virginia, with the primary mission of defending Virginia against invasion. He lacked the authority, the information, the point of vantage, and the breadth of mission for putting into effect such a plan as he expounded. The supreme weakness of Confederate operations in the summer of 1863 was not the offensive into Pennsylvania: it was the want of a unified command and strategy. As a result, no adequate strategic reserve was ever created out of the minor departments: the weak reserve that was formed was sent to Mississippi, while the main effort of the Confederacy was made in Pennsylvania. The right hand knew not what the left hand was about.

Let us deal the cards in Lee's favor, as they are often dealt in favor of the hypothetical plans that he opposed, and for a moment speculate on what might have been, had he been authentic general-in-chief in early 1863. Lee would have stripped the minor departments of troops, save for minimum defensive garrisons, and from this source would have strengthened the main effort of the Confederacy. He would have given Joseph E. Johnston full authority in Mississippi, and would have ordered a concentrated effort against Grant there. Lee would have ordered Bragg to strike again into Kentucky in order to draw Rosecrans out of Tennessee and alarm the authorities and people of the North. Lee would have placed Beauregard with an army in effigy to threaten Washington from the South and paralyze his opponent. Lee would have led the Army of Northern Virginia, powerfully reinforced, into Pennsylvania. Lee would have kept his cavalry in hand, and would have discovered and destroyed Meade's two advance corps at Gettysburg on July 1, before the rest of the Northern army could reach the battlefield. With his opponents scattered, confused, and demoralized, Lee would have struck the final psychological blow at the Northern will: he would have offered a negotiated peace with a hint that the Union might thus be preserved. Given all of these conditions, the Gettysburg campaign was perhaps as likely to end the war successfully for the South as was any other strategy.

But enough of make-believe: campaigns are seldom waged as critics afterward would have them waged.

During the months after Gettysburg, Lee continued to believe that even yet he might be able to invade the North successfully. But defeat in Pennsylvania left its mark on him: when, upon Meade's failing to press Lee, Davis again desired to send a part of Lee's troops west, Lee consented. In early September he dispatched Longstreet with 12,000 men to strengthen Bragg's army before Chattanooga. Victory at Chickamauga in mid-September was followed by disaster at Chattanooga in November. Weakened by Longstreet's absence, Lee made one unsuccessful offensive effort against Meade (Bristoe Station, October 14), then fell back on the defensive.

Lee now knew that the South was too weak to invade the North. Loss of Chattanooga moved him again to write Davis concerning the general Confederate military situation. The Union army at Chattanooga now threatens Georgia with her factories and provisions, Lee said; it must be stopped if the Confederacy is to survive. Place Beauregard in command of the Confederate army in Georgia, and reinforce him with troops from Mississippi, Mobile, and Charleston, urged Lee. To defeat the coming Federal move, he explained, "the safety of points practically less important than those endangered by [it] must be hazarded. Upon the defence of the country threatened by [the enemy march] depends the safety of the points now held by us on the Atlantic, and they are in as great danger from [a] successful advance as by the attacks to which they are at present subjected." Written four months before Sherman set forth to destroy the war support of the lower South, these words show profound insight into the deficiencies of Confederate strategy. They were a prophecy of total war uttered out of season.[24]

Spring of 1864 brought face to face the military giants of the Civil War, Lee and Grant. Now came the heaviest sustained fighting that American troops have ever experienced. True to their natures and to their philosophies of war, both men attempted to seize the initiative in order to destroy the other. As Grant advanced below the Rapidan, Lee attacked fiercely. Had the two forces been equal in numbers, Lee may have achieved his aim, for he took Grant at disadvantage on the march in a country of woods and bramble. But the forces were not equal. For two days in the battle of the Wilderness (May 5–6) the result trembled in the balance as both forces fought desperately for survival. Then the armies broke off action, neither of them victorious. Sensing his opponent's tenacity and purpose, Lee now moved unerringly to block Grant's circling advance against the flank and rear of the Army of Northern Virginia.

Failure to destroy or stop Grant in the Wilderness marked the beginning of a new phase in Lee's career. He continued to seek favorable opportunity to strike Grant, for Lee had long said that his army would be lost if ever it should be pinned down in the Richmond defenses. But the Wilderness was Lee's last general offensive action; the Army of Northern Virginia no longer had the power to attack. Hoping yet to demoralize the people of the North and place the peace party there in the ascendancy, Lee husbanded his waning strength and sought to exact of Grant the maximum toll in blood and energy. When one lacks the strength to destroy the enemy, says Clausewitz, then one ought, by skillful conservation of his own resources, to seek to exhaust the enemy's will by showing him that the cost of victory far exceeds his anticipation.[25] Lee's strategy was now the strategy of conservation.

For more than a week of fierce but intermittent fighting at Spotsylvania Courthouse (May 8–18) Grant hammered at Lee's line. Unable to break it, Grant moved again. Repeatedly he sideslipped to the left and inched forward in an effort to encircle Lee's flank, force him out of position, and destroy him.

Repeatedly Lee anticipated his opponent's move and shifted athwart the flanking column. From Spotsylvania Courthouse to the North Anna River, and from there to Cold Harbor veered the deadly grapple. Earthworks went up at every position. At Cold Harbor (June 3) Grant again drove his battering-ram against the Southern line. Reinforced with troops rushed from minor Confederate victories in the Shenandoah Valley and on the James River below Richmond, Lee repulsed the Northern assault with fearful punishment. Voices of censure began to rise against Grant "the butcher" among the civil and military population of the North. After a month of bloodshed such as the American people had never seen, the Army of the Potomac was still farther from Richmond than McClellan had been in the summer of 1862: Lee's gaunt army was still apparently invincible.[26]

Lee used his great talents to the utmost during this month of remorseless combat. His ability to foresee and counteract enemy strategy has become a part of universal military tradition. Carefully fitting together the shards of information collected from the battlefield, from prisoners, and from scouts and spies, Lee supplied the gaps from his own intellect and intuition: out of the whole he created a true mosaic of enemy intentions. Then he was bold enough to trust his judgment and to act accordingly. Lee must be a great strategist, wrote a Michigan soldier; for everywhere the Northern army goes, it finds the Rebels already there. To friend and foe alike, Lee's skill seemed miraculous.[27]

With remarkable effectiveness, Lee made capital of the advantages inherent in the defense. His tactical employment of interior lines enabled him to move more quickly than did his opponent from one position to another. On a larger scale, he used interior lines to draw reinforcements from the Shenandoah Valley and the Peninsula; thus he partially offset the unavoidable handicap of fighting with flank and rear exposed to a sea controlled by the enemy. Relying upon the increased firepower of Civil War weapons, and ignoring Jomini's contempt for prepared positions, Lee developed the science of field fortification to a degree that significantly altered modern defensive tactics; he elevated axe and spade to near-equality with musket and howitzer.

Lee's choice of position was unimpeachable; his eye for ground unerring. "When his eye swept a countryside it never betrayed him," says Cyril Falls. "From the ground or the map, or both in combination, [Lee] realized how to make the best use of every feature of the country, and the trace of every defensive position from his hand was masterly." Sound position, strengthened by field fortification, enabled Lee at critical moments to flout the tactical rule that one must always keep a reserve in being; he achieved maximum firepower by placing every regiment on the line. "If I shorten my lines to provide a reserve he will turn me," Lee told an observer at Cold Harbor. "If I weaken them to provide a reserve, he will break me." Audacity thus met the summons of necessity.[28]

Students of Lee's conduct in this campaign find it a brilliant lesson in defensive warfare. "[It] is a classical example in military history of how these objects [conserving one's own strength and taxing that of the enemy] ought to be sought," says Sir Frederic Maurice. "In method it was fifty years ahead of the times, and I believe that if the allies in August, 1914, had applied Lee's tactical methods to the situation . . . the course of the World War [I] would have been changed."[29]

Having failed to break Lee at Cold Harbor, Grant on June 12–16 marched around Richmond on the east and struck at Lee's communications by attacking the Petersburg rail junction below Richmond. As Grant half-circled Richmond, Lee warily moved along an inner half circle that kept his army between Grant and the city. This enabled Grant to pass south of the James River and fall with overwhelming force upon the defend-

ers of Petersburg under Beauregard. Grant's move was daring
in concept and skillful in execution. For several days Lee lost
touch with the Army of the Potomac. But Grant's attack at
Petersburg wanted the skill of his march. Beauregard held
the Northern army at bay, and on June 18 Lee hastened the
Army of Northern Virginia into the Petersburg trenches where
the great siege of the war began.

Lee shrewdly anticipated Grant's move south of the James;
before Grant left Cold Harbor, Lee predicted such an attempt.
Aware that he could not indefinitely withstand the full weight
of Grant's numbers, which would grow with time, Lee sought
again to weaken Grant's main body by creating a diversion
elsewhere. Should he succeed in this, Lee hoped to be able to
strike a telling blow at the force still opposing him. He hoped
to repeat the maneuver that had caused a diversion of troops
from McClellan's Peninsula army in the summer of 1862. Lee
knew that Grant would not be shaken by this ruse. Lee's strategy was aimed above Grant's head; it was aimed at Lincoln
himself. On June 13, the day on which Lee learned that Grant's
army was no longer before him at Cold Harbor, Lee sent General Jubal Early with 13,000 men to threaten Washington from
the Shenandoah Valley.

Notwithstanding Lee's foresight, and in spite of General
Beauregard's many warnings and pleas for reinforcement, Lee
responded slowly to Grant's move away from Cold Harbor.
Lee's tardiness has some justification; it was the result of a
narrow mission and of his want of information on the whereabouts of Grant's army. Lee's primary mission was to protect
the capital; without accurate knowledge of Grant's location,
Lee thought it hazardous to uncover the direct route to the
city. Confederate cavalry was absent, defending the Virginia
Central Railroad against a massive Union cavalry raid. Beauregard's cries for help gave Lee no accurate information about
the enemy; not until June 17 did Beauregard report that the

Army of the Potomac was south of the James. Nevertheless, Lee did permit Grant to make the maneuver to Petersburg without striking him while on the march and vulnerable; and Lee did fail to checkmate the move at Petersburg until almost too late. Beauregard's determined resistance there saved the vital rail junction from capture. One must conclude that Grant was at his best in the passage of the James, while Lee's performance here was below that of the Wilderness–to–Cold Harbor campaign.[30]

The siege of Petersburg lasted almost nine months. It was so long and costly that it seriously blighted Northern morale; it brought to the South a false hope of ultimate success. Sherman was now halted before Atlanta, and the end of the war appeared nowhere in sight. The peace movement in the North was growing. President Lincoln himself believed his re-election to the presidency unlikely; if his Democratic opponent, General McClellan, should be victorious on a peace platform, said Lincoln, the Union probably could not be restored. Lee now learned that Davis was about to relieve Joseph E. Johnston from command of the Confederate army at Atlanta. Again Lee offered advice on general Confederate strategy. If Davis felt it necessary to remove Johnston, said Lee, then it must be done; but Lee made clear his own aversion to the decision. "It is a grievous thing to change the commander of an army situated as [the Army of Tennessee is]," he said. He had hoped that Johnston was strong enough to fight for Atlanta, wrote Lee; which was his way of saying that battle ought to be risked in an effort to save the city. If not, he counseled, concentrate all cavalry in the west on Sherman's communications, and let the Confederate army fall back upon Augusta. This was probably as wise a move as the Confederacy was capable of making at this time.[31]

Lee's demonstration against Washington failed to break Grant's hold at Petersburg. Response of the Union authorities showed that Lee's instinct was sound. As General Early crossed the Potomac and threatened Washington during the first week of July, General Halleck called upon Grant for troops; and on July 10, President Lincoln recommended, though he did not order it, that Grant himself come to the capital with a portion of the Army of the Potomac. But Lee wanted the strength to take advantage of his opponent's dispersals. Ultimately, Grant sent into the Valley enough troops to defeat Early; but Grant kept in the Petersburg entrenchments enough men to render an attack there by Lee impossible. Either Lee must hold his lines at Petersburg to the bitter end, or he must abandon Richmond altogether.

Doubtless Richmond ought now, at all hazard, to have been given up. Atlanta was lost on September 2; its fall assured Lincoln's re-election to the presidency and doomed the Northern peace movement. Lee could not hope to destroy or seriously cripple Grant's army: Hood's effort to stop Sherman had ended in disaster. Perhaps the only remote chance of Confederate survival was for Lee to break away from Grant and attempt junction with Hood somewhere in the lower South for alternate blows, first against Sherman and then against Grant. That this would have brought deliverance to the stricken Confederacy is, of course, well-nigh inconceivable: it would have meant the immediate loss of the entire east; and Sherman's army could have been promptly reinforced to a strength that would have rendered him secure even against such combined attack. Lee saw the futility of trying to hold Richmond any longer. He had long said that a siege would destroy his army; that it must remain free to maneuver and strike if it were to live in the presence of so powerful a foe. In October, probably after the final defeat of Early in the Valley, Lee told his staff officers that Richmond was a millstone to his army. But the decision to abandon Richmond was not Lee's to make. Only Davis could make it: and Lee's exaggerated deference to the President and

Commander-in-Chief would not permit him to suggest it as long as the city's defense was the first mission of his army.[32]

Hunger, cold, disease, and heartache over the plight of distant loved ones: these immeasurably assisted Grant's shells during the winter of 1864–65 to break Lee's army in flesh and spirit. Still his troops held grimly to the Petersburg defenses. In early February, under heavy public pressure, the Confederate Congress created the position of general-in-chief: though Davis rightly interpreted this as a vote of censure against his leadership, he appointed Lee to the post.

As general-in-chief, Lee held dubious rank. President Davis had once written to Lee, "I have neither the [constitutional] power nor the will to delegate" to someone else the supreme command. In appointing Grant to command all Union forces, President Lincoln said to him, "The particulars of your plan I neither know nor seek to know. . . . I wish not to obtrude any constraints or restraints upon you. . . ." Such a letter as Lincoln's is unimaginable from Davis. When General Joseph E. Johnston heard of Lee's appointment as general-in-chief, Johnston wrote perceptively, "Do not expect much of Lee in this capacity. He cannot give up the command of the Army of Northern Virginia without becoming merely a minor official. . . ." No man could with impunity trespass upon Davis' authority; for Lee to attempt it would have been futile. Through tact and suggestion Lee accomplished far more with Davis than he could have accomplished in any other way. Lee thus saved his talents, though circumscribed, for the Confederacy: others, such as Beauregard and Joseph E. Johnston, who sought through sharper methods to influence Davis, wasted their faculties during most of the war in idleness and frustration. As long as Davis was president of the Confederacy he would be commander-in-chief in fact as in law.[33]

Only by the most drastic means could Lee have made his

new authority tell. Only by a passionate appeal, in his own name, to the spirit of the South; only by commandeering railroads and provisions; only by abandoning Richmond, if possible, in order to concentrate against fractions of the enemy: in sum, only by making himself dictator in the manner of ancient Rome could Lee possibly have prolonged the life of the dying Confederacy. Prolonged it for a brief season, that is; for at this stage nothing could have postponed the final outcome for very long. Lee knew what measures were required: he discussed them with his staff and others. Doubtless the Congress and people of the South would have supported him in these moves. But Lee would not take them.

In accepting the appointment as general-in-chief, Lee made clear that he would continue to operate under Davis' authority. Lee is often censured for this subordination to Davis. Lee's adjutant general admitted that this deference robbed Lee of the qualities of a revolutionary leader.[34] But it is one thing to criticize Lee as a revolutionary: it is quite another thing to disparage Lee's generalship. Subordination of the military to the civil authorities is usually deemed a virtue among Americans: George Washington shunned the temptation to grasp the reins of government at dark moments during the War for Independence; nothing in Grant's career indicates that he would have led a coup d'état against President Lincoln if he had thought Lincoln a bungler. Indeed, Grant probably was as submissive to Lincoln as was Lee to Davis. To Grant's admirers, Lee's submissiveness was servility, while Grant's submissiveness was military statesmanship. Modern scholars who condemn Lee for his subordination to Davis look with indignation upon an American general who dared defy his President and Commander-in-Chief in a recent war. Lee was too American to play Napoleon.

Nevertheless, rather through suggestion than through command, Lee as general-in-chief attempted certain broad, co-ordinated strategic measures. He brought Joseph E. Johnston out of idleness and sent him to North Carolina to oppose Sherman; Lee ordered Johnston to collect for this effort all the scattered troops of the Confederacy, except the Army of Northern Virginia. Lee advised the War Department that he must now unite his own force with that of Johnston, though this would forfeit the capital. Hoping to strike a concerted blow against Sherman, then one against Grant, Lee began to prepare supply depots for a march to the south.[35]

But such a move was impossible through the mud of winter and with horses near starvation: Lee must wait for the roads to dry and for his livestock to regain strength. Lee must also win Davis to the desperate plan. The President blew hot and cold on it: previously he had hinted that all of the cities of the South might have to be given up in the waging of the war; now in early March he approved Lee's strategy of joining forces with Johnston. But Davis never gave unqualified consent to the abandonment of the capital; he never fully prepared himself to leave. On April 1, the day before Lee was driven from the Petersburg line, someone asked Davis whether Richmond would be held. "[Yes] If we can," replied the indomitable Mississippian.[36]

As commander of the Army of Northern Virginia, Lee strove mightily during these last days just to keep his army alive: hunger, exposure, demoralization, and constant attack by Grant's well-fed and well-clad army rendered this a burden beyond description. That, under these conditions, Lee was able to maintain a cohesive fighting force through the winter of 1864–65 is an enduring tribute to his leadership.

As general-in-chief, Lee devoted his thought to disengaging his army from Grant's tentacles and moving south to join Johnston. To combine the armies against Sherman would be a prodigious feat. It required far more than simply moving the Army of Northern Virginia from Petersburg to North Carolina, though this alone would have taxed grievously the waning resources of the Confederacy. To accomplish the junction, Lee must free himself from Grant; then Lee's famished and exhausted troops must outmarch Grant's vigorous army. Moreover, since Grant's line enveloped Lee on the south, and the direct route to North Carolina (the Weldon Railroad) was in Grant's control, Lee had to move farther to escape than did Grant to block the escape. Lee must march west and then turn south, describing two sides of a triangle, while to intercept this movement, Grant need only proceed along the third side of the triangle. Lee intended to do all in his power to make the junction; but he rightly sensed that it was well-nigh impossible. Since the coming of winter, quite likely no man or measure could have freed the Army of Northern Virginia from the Army of the Potomac, competently led.

On March 25, Lee made his move to escape and join Johnston. In an effort to force Grant to withdraw his encircling troops from the southern end of the line, Lee attacked Fort Stedman east of Petersburg. Lee planned then to slip away and gain a march on his adversary in the deadly race. Probably no better strategy could have been devised. But the attempt failed; Lee's army was too weak to break Grant's fortified line. Grant countered instantly with a successful thrust at Five Forks on the Southside Railroad (April 1): Lee's last line of supply was severed. The next day he abandoned Petersburg and marched west for the Danville Railroad, which would carry him roundabout to junction with Johnston's army. Lee gained the railroad at Amelia Courthouse, only to lose a precious day there because his order for rations had gone awry. Before he could move south, Grant blocked the railroad at Burkeville. Lee then pushed west again, hoping somewhere to be able to turn the corner and get south of Grant's army. All was futile: outpaced and surrounded, Lee ended the terrible drama on April 9 in the surrender of his army.[37]

At last Lee's sword was sheathed.

*   *   *   *   *   *   *   *   *

For near a century, most students of the art of war have looked with unqualified admiration upon the generalship of Lee. Early Northern historians of the Civil War lavished praise upon him: James Ford Rhodes attributed chiefly to Lee's talents the South's unsurpassed power of resistance; John C. Ropes said of Lee, "No army commander on either side was so universally believed in, so absolutely trusted. Nor was there ever a commander who better deserved the support of his Government and the affection and confidence of his soldiers." General Viscount Wolseley of England believed that Lee was the most skillful of American generals. Colonel G. F. R. Henderson, one of the nineteenth century's most perceptive military analysts, called Lee "one of the greatest, if not the greatest, soldier who ever spoke the English tongue." Sir Frederic Maurice, critic of strategy both ancient and modern, placed Lee among the most illustrious commanders of the ages. After studying the careers of the most renowned generals of the last hundred years, Cyril Falls concludes that Lee is the greatest of them all. "Lee alone in a century of warfare deserves to be ranked with Hannibal and Napoleon," says Falls. Dennis W. Brogan, keenest of present European students of American history, says that Lee was the supreme military leader of the Civil War. Grant's solutions were adequate but seldom elegant, says Brogan; Lee's solutions were frequently elegant. The man who is perhaps today's greatest living scholar-warrior and surest connoisseur of military leadership seconds these exalted estimates of Lee. Winston Churchill writes, "Lee was one of the greatest captains known to the annals of war."[38]

Critics arise from time to time to challenge the grounds of Lee's fame. They have found human failings in him; but frequently their complaints against his generalship cancel one another out. Lee was too rash and combative, says one: Lee was excessively slow and cautious, says another. Lee did not take advantage of the South's interior lines, says one: Lee clung to the obsolete concept of interior lines, says another. Lee failed to concentrate the forces of the Confederacy, says one: Lee was preoccupied with the outworn principle of concentration, says another. Lee was a slave to Jomini, says one: Lee violated Jomini's fundamental principle of war, says another. Criticism of Lee thus often ends in a confusion of tongues.

Certainly Lee was mortal: notwithstanding remarkable accomplishments, his military leadership fell short of the abstract yardstick of perfection. Major criticisms of Lee as a strategist have already been considered in this essay: that he was too provincial to see the war as a whole, and too conservative to break the fetters of the past. Without laboring all of the minor criticisms of Lee, a few may be scrutinized here.[39]

It has been said that Lee did not see the relationship between strategy and statecraft in modern war. This is true in that Lee deferred excessively to Davis and refused to seize dictatorial authority in a belated effort to save the Confederacy. But on a higher plane the criticism is not true. Lee's foresight regarding the nature and magnitude of the war; his prescience in urging total mobilization; his prediction that Europe would remain aloof from the war; his adaptation of abstract military theory to the exigencies of Southern politics, economics, and logistics; his strategies aimed as well at President Lincoln's fears as at the weaknesses of opposing generals; his suggestions of peace overtures to encourage the Northern peace movement and split the mind of the enemy; and his advocacy of the employment of Negro troops and their subsequent emancipation: all argue that Lee saw far beyond the battlefield in waging war. Lee seasoned military strategy with a rich wisdom and insight into human affairs that transcended statecraft in its primal sense to become true statesmanship.

Lee is sometimes disparaged for the slack discipline of his command; certainly, by professional standards, or by twentieth-century standards in citizen armies, discipline in the Army of Northern Virginia was easy. Yet one may question whether any other method of managing the army would have accomplished as much. To be of value, discipline must be suited to the character of the men, says Sir Frederic Maurice. "Lee knew well that the discipline of Frederick [the Great's] grenadiers" would destroy his army of highly individualistic Southern planters and farmers. "The object of discipline in an army is to give bodies of men both cohesion and the instinct to suffer all for duty in circumstances of great stress and danger," explains Maurice. Few armies, if any, have ever endured more steadfastly the stress of privation and the danger of combat than did the Army of Northern Virginia.[40]

Lee's most unsparing critic, General J. F. C. Fuller, heaps scorn upon Lee as being a poor provider for his army. But General Fuller offers no promising remedy for the ills of the Confederate quartermaster and commissary. Lee kept every wheel turning, and the wires hot with dispatches; he scattered his troops among the fields and flocks of the Southern countryside, often at the expense of combat efficiency; and he sometimes launched invasions of the well-stocked North: all in a ceaseless effort to feed and clothe his men. How, under the circumstances, anyone else in Lee's position could have done better is beyond convincing explanation.

Lee is sometimes taken to task for his extreme combativeness, his lust for battle for its own sake. "It is well that war is so terrible," said Lee while surveying the carnage before his position at Fredericksburg, "else we should grow too fond of it." This trait perhaps unsettled Lee's judgment on the third day of Gettysburg and caused him to attempt the impossible. But the will to fight is a fault easily forgiven in a warrior. Too often the critics believe that wars are won in some manner other than that by which they must be won, says Cyril Falls, which is by fighting. "Happy the army in which an untimely boldness frequently manifests itself," wrote Clausewitz. Lee's "fighting blood" (as Freeman calls it) was one of the qualities that made him formidable. If, on occasion, it betrayed him into unwise combat, on many others it saved him. It helped to make him, in the words of an opponent, "a very thunderbolt in war."

General Fuller believes that Lee failed to stamp his mind upon his military operations. Oddly, if Lee did not stamp his mind upon his own operations, he stamped it powerfully upon the operations of his enemy. "Among the many achievements of this remarkable man [Lee]," writes Bruce Catton, "nothing is more striking than his ability to dominate the minds of the men who were fighting against him." Lee's campaigns were the very product of his mind. One had as well say that the frescoes of the Sistine Chapel want the stamp of Michelangelo's mind as that the operations of the Army of Northern Virginia want the stamp of Lee's mind.[41]

Under the travail of his command, Lee sometimes made unaccountable errors of judgment regarding enemy capabilities outside his own department. His belief that the summer climate of Mississippi would stop Grant at Vicksburg; and his doubt that Sherman could march through the Carolinas: these were wide of the mark. But they were offered as mere opinions. Significantly, they did not alter Lee's strategy: notwithstanding his notions, Lee urged that Joseph E. Johnston concentrate and attack Grant in Mississippi without delay; and later Lee ordered Johnston to oppose Sherman's drive in North Carolina with every man available to the embattled Confederacy.

Perhaps the chief flaw in Lee's generalship came of his boundless courtesy and humility. These traits heightened his deference to President Davis; sometimes they weakened Lee's supremacy over his army. Lee chose rather to lead through tact and orders of discretion than through iron discipline and positive commands. Freeman believes that at times Lee even permitted himself to be browbeaten by a stubborn subordinate. Yet the critic must be careful in scoring Lee on this count; some of Lee's most spectacular victories were the result of discretionary instructions to resourceful corps commanders. Ideally, Lee ought to have known to give Jackson his head, but to keep tight rein on Stuart and Ewell; to stir Gordon with quiet suggestion, but to impel Longstreet with sharp command. Here Lee made the mistake of attributing to all of his lieutenants his own great tactical insight and high code of gentlemanly attitude.[42]

Lee's theory of battlefield command did not always measure up to his other qualities of leadership. To fashion strategy and so manage his army as to bring it with maximum efficiency to the point of decision: this, felt Lee, was his primary function. Once the missions were assigned and the battle joined, he sometimes permitted control to drift. He was most guilty of this on the second day of Gettysburg: here, for a time, says Freeman, the Army of Northern Virginia was virtually without a commander. Lee remedied this mistake during the later campaigns of the war.[43]

In dwelling upon Lee's particular weaknesses and misjudgments, both real and imagined, critics obscure his achievements as a whole. As commander of the Army of Northern Virginia, Lee's sole responsibility throughout most of the war, he earned the acclaim of history. Circumscribed in command, opposing overwhelming numbers, and fighting under every material disadvantage known to the science of war, Lee through his generalship largely sustained the Confederacy in one of the most prodigious military efforts of the modern age. What he could have accomplished as untrammeled general-in-chief must remain conjecture. His actual accomplishments, all things considered, were second to none in the American military experience. His virtues as a general transcended his faults.

Lee's prime quality, according to Freeman, was intellect; it was "the accurate reasoning of a trained and precise mind"; it was a "developed aptitude for the difficult synthesis of war." Intellect of the highest order enabled Lee to look into his opponents' minds and read their intentions, doubts, and fears; then with maximum efficiency to capitalize upon this knowledge.[44]

Audacity enhanced intellect to make Lee the general. Boldness is the noblest of military virtues, says Clausewitz; it is the "true steel which gives the weapon its edge and brilliancy. . . . Boldness, directed by an overruling intelligence, is the stamp of the hero." Audacity enabled Lee repeatedly to seize the initiative from opponents commanding twice his strength; audacity moved him time and again to flout the established rules of warfare in order to strike the foe at the least expected times and places. "We must decide between the positive loss of inactivity and the risk of action," Lee once wrote in a terse but profound exposition of his theory of war. Lee's prowess came largely of a readiness to accept the risk of action.[45]

Character exalted intellect and audacity to make Lee one of the greatest leaders of men the world has known. "Alexander, Hannibal, Caesar . . . and Napoleon [had] the highest faculties of mind," says F. E. Adcock in a study on the outstanding generals of antiquity. "But . . . they possessed character in a still greater degree. To this list," continues Adcock, "I would add . . . Robert E. Lee." Character lights the moral flame of leadership, a quality indefinable and mysterious, one that Clausewitz says can be spoken of only in words vague and rhapsodical. Deep religious conviction united with the chivalric tradition of Virginia aristocracy to endow Lee with remarkable serenity and nobility of nature. "I have met many of the great men of my time," said General Viscount Wolseley, "but Lee alone impressed me with the feeling that I was in the presence of a man who was cast in a grander mould, and made of different and finer metal than all other men. He is stamped upon my memory as a being apart and superior to all others in every way: a man with whom none I ever knew, a very few of whom I have ever read, are worthy to be classed." Lee's sharpest critic eloquently tells the effect of Lee's leadership through character. "Few generals," writes General Fuller, "have been able to animate an army as [Lee's] self-sacrificing idealism animated the Army of Northern Virginia. . . . What this bootless, ragged, half-starved army accomplished is one of the miracles of history."[46]

Times are perilously late for Americans to permit the zeal of nationalism to blind them to excellence, no matter whence it may come. Lee's career teaches certain lessons for the military leadership of today. Jet airplanes, intercontinental missiles, and thermonuclear bombs make the weapons of Lee's era as obsolete as the tomahawk; they bring war to hypertrophy. But if today's "balance of terror" should continue to prevail, and mankind be spared the fiery bolts of extinction, then Lee's strategic and tactical concepts will again prove useful in the employment of conventional military forces. Victory through attrition, which has been the key to American strategy in the Civil War and the two world wars, is no longer possible for this nation; nor can she hope to destroy the war strength of her opponents without resort to thermonuclear weapons. She must again learn the skills of swift maneuver and the delivery of paralyzing blows by highly mobile forces upon lines of communication and points of decision. Armies of the future must be composed of semi-independent, self-contained units, says General Matthew Ridgway, units capable of operating over great distances on a fluid battlefield, and with a minimum of control from higher headquarters.[47] These words remind one of Lee's discretionary orders to the virtually independent commanders, Jackson, Stuart, Early, and at the end, Joseph E. Johnston. In darker extremity, this nation must again learn to wage cunning defensive war for the conservation of weaker resources: war that destroys the enemy's resolve by taxing him beyond his anticipation.

Finally, if this people must fight again, either with conventional arms or in the holocaust of thermonuclear war, then the nobler qualities of Lee's generalship will offer an even brighter example than his techniques of combat. Intellect to divine and cope with enemy capabilities and intentions; boldness to strike when the occasion demands, however grave the risk; and above all, character to inspire purpose and sacrifice in the midst of supreme stress, hardship, and danger: these will be the imperatives of leadership for national survival. The art and science of war can yet profit from the genius of Lee.

NOTES

1. Carl Von Clausewitz, *On War* (3 vols.; London and New York, 1940), I, 194–95, III, 170–71.

2. Charles P. Roland, *The Confederacy* (Chicago, 1960), 34–41.

3. J. F. C. Fuller, *Grant and Lee* (Bloomington, 1957), 262.

4. Cyril Falls, *A Hundred Years of War* (London, 1953), 18; Archer Jones, *Confederate Strategy from Shiloh to Vicksburg* (Baton Rouge, 1961), 16–32.

5. Fuller, *Grant and Lee,* 39–40; Charles de Gaulle, *The Edge of the Sword* (New York, 1960), 93–94; Frederic Maurice, *Robert E. Lee the Soldier* (Boston and New York, 1925), 76.

6. Douglas Southall Freeman, *R. E. Lee* (4 vols.; New York and London, 1934–35), II, 6–7.

7. *Ibid.,* I, 621.

8. Lee to Albert Sidney Johnston, March 26, 1862, in Mrs. Mason Barret Collection of Albert Sidney and William Preston Johnston Papers (Tulane University Archives, New Orleans).

9. Freeman, *R. E. Lee,* II, 28.

10. Niccolò Machiavelli, *The Art of War* (Albany, 1815), 233; Freeman, *R. E. Lee,* II, 39–50, 53–57.

11. Freeman, *R. E. Lee,* II, 199.

12. Clausewitz, *On War,* I, 100; Freeman, *R. E. Lee,* II, 302, 256–349.

The Generalship of Robert E. Lee

13. G. F. R. Henderson, *The Science of War* (London and New York, 1905), 175; R. Ernest Dupuy and Trevor N. Dupuy, *The Compact History of the Civil War* (New York, 1960), 156–57.

14. David Donald, *Lincoln Reconsidered* (New York, 1956), 94; T. Harry Williams, "The Military Leadership of North and South," in David Donald (ed.), *Why the North Won the Civil War* (Baton Rouge, 1960), 32; Clausewitz, *On War*, II, 154–55.

15. Clausewitz, *On War*, I, 35, 174.

16. Freeman, *R. E. Lee*, III, 34.

17. Henderson, *The Science of War*, 35.

18. Jones, *Confederate Strategy from Shiloh to Vicksburg*, 211–13; Freeman, *R. E. Lee*, III, 29–161.

19. Williams, "The Military Leadership of North and South," in Donald (ed.), *Why the North Won the Civil War*, 40, 46.

20. E. P. Alexander, *Military Memoirs of a Confederate* (New York, 1908), 364–65.

21. Walter Millis, *Arms and Men* (New York, 1956), 111.

22. Gordon A. Harrison, *Cross Channel Attack* (Washington, 1951), 76; Forrest C. Pogue, *The Supreme Command* (Washington, 1954), 182–83. Both of these volumes are in the *United States Army in World War II* series, prepared by the Office of the Chief of Military History, Department of the Army.

23. Jones, *Confederate Strategy from Shiloh to Vicksburg*, 24–25.

24. Freeman, *R. E. Lee*, III, 206–07.

25. Clausewitz, *On War*, I, 35.

26. Freeman, *R. E. Lee*, III, 275–391; Bruce Catton, *A Stillness at Appomattox* (New York, 1958), 63–187.

27. Catton, *A Stillness at Appomattox*, 152.

28. Falls, *A Hundred Years of War*, 59–60; Alfred H. Burne, *Lee, Grant and Sherman* (New York, 1939), 49.

29. Maurice, *Robert E. Lee the Soldier*, 85.

30. Burne, *Lee, Grant and Sherman*, 55–61; Freeman, *R. E. Lee*, III, 392–447.

31. Freeman, *R. E. Lee*, III, 461–62.

32. *Ibid.*, 441, 496n; Walter H. Taylor, *Four Years with General Lee* (New York, 1878), 145.

33. Jones, *Confederate Strategy from Shiloh to Vicksburg*, 232; Dupuy and Dupuy, *The Compact History of the Civil War*, 281; Gilbert E. Govan and James W. Livingood, *A Different Valor* (New York, 1956), 343.

34. Taylor, *Four Years with General Lee*, 148.

35. Govan and Livingood, *A Different Valor*, 347.

36. Varina Howell Davis, *Jefferson Davis: A Memoir by His Wife* (2 vols.; New York, 1890), II, 579.

37. Freeman, *R. E. Lee*, IV, 1–143.

38. Burne, *Lee, Grant and Sherman*, 207; John C. Ropes, *The Story of the Civil War* (4 vols.; New York, 1933), II, 157–58; Garnet J. Wolseley,

General Lee (Rochester, 1906), 62; Henderson, *The Science of War*, 314; Maurice, *Robert E. Lee the Soldier*, 293–94; Falls, *A Hundred Years of War*, 48; D. W. Brogan, "A Fresh Appraisal of the Civil War," *Harper's Magazine* (April, 1960), 136; Winston Churchill, *A History of the English Speaking People* (4 vols.; New York, 1958), IV, 169.

39. The most sweeping criticisms of Lee's generalship are in Fuller, *Grant and Lee*. Other sharp criticisms are in Donald, *Lincoln Reconsidered*, 82–102; and Williams, "The Military Leadership of North and South," in Donald (ed.), *Why the North Won the Civil War*, 23–47.

40. Maurice, *Robert E. Lee the Soldier*, 162–63.

41. Catton, *A Stillness at Appomattox*, 48.

42. Freeman, *R. E. Lee*, IV, 168.

43. *Ibid.*, 168–69.

44. *Ibid.*, 170–73.

45. Clausewitz, *On War*, I, 188–91; Freeman, *R. E. Lee*, IV, 172.

46. F. E. Adcock, *The Greek and Macedonian Art of War* (Berkeley, 1957), 83; Clausewitz, *On War*, I, 178–79; Wolseley, *General Lee*, 60–61; Fuller, *Grant and Lee*, 280, 117.

47. Quoted in Millis, *Arms and Men*, 318.

Devils Facing Zionwards

by DAVID DONALD

I

MOST CIVIL WAR HISTORY is written in clichés. We still speak
of the conflict as a war between North and South, though everybody knows that there was much pro-Confederate sentiment in
the Union, that four Southern states never seceded, and that even
in the deep South there was resistance to Jefferson Davis' government. We write of a struggle between freedom and slavery,
even though the Confederates were prepared to free their slaves
before the North was ready to adopt the Thirteenth Amendment. Military historians oppose the Clausewitzian theories of
General Grant to the old-fashioned strategy of Robert E. Lee,
although these two great generals were trained in the same
school and shared virtually all the same ideas about warfare.

In the political history of the Civil War one of the most
widely held of these stereotypes is the cliché of Lincoln versus
the Radicals.[1] The most serious opponents of President Lincoln,
so the story goes, were not the Democrats or even the Confederates but the "Jacobin" members of his own party. "Aggressive,
vindictive, and narrowly sectional," these Radicals "welcomed
the outbreak of civil war as the longed-for opportunity to
destroy slavery and to drive the 'slave traders' from the national temple." Once the war came, they stood "for instant
emancipation, the confiscation of 'rebel' property, the use of
colored soldiers, civil and, when it should become expedient,
political equality for the Negro." Behind their antislavery zeal
lay their desire to "fasten Republican political and economic
control upon the South"; they expected to enact a high protec-

tive tariff that would foster monopoly, to pass a homestead law that would invite speculators to loot the public domain, and to subsidize a transcontinental railroad that would offer infinite opportunities for jobbery. Before the war Southern planters had been the chief obstacle in the path of their plans. Now that the Southerners had withdrawn from the Union, the Radicals vowed never to readmit them until their political and economic power was broken. As Wendell Phillips pledged, "The whole social system of the Gulf states is to be taken to pieces; every bit of it."

The Conservative President of the United States, so the cliché runs, opposed these schemes. Lincoln was determined to keep the Civil War from becoming a social revolution. As genuinely antislavery as the Radicals, he advocated the "gradual extinction of slavery, compensated emancipation, and colonization of the Negroes in another land." He looked for a prompt restoration of the seceded states to the Union.

Master politicians, the Radicals skillfully undermined the President's program. They hounded his military and civilian advisers who did not share their Radical views. Fearing that General George B. McClellan would end the war without ending slavery, they worked assiduously for his removal from command; similarly in the west they secured the dismissal of Don Carlos Buell. Of the members of the cabinet they unsparingly denounced Seward, Bates, and Welles, and they forced the resignation of Montgomery Blair. Toward the President himself their hostility was unceasing. The bolder among them sneered at him as a baboon; others characterized his administration as being marked by "epaulettes and apathy, imbecility and treachery, idiocy and ignorance, sacrifice on the part of the people, supineness on the part of the Government." [2] They vigorously opposed the renomination of Lincoln in 1864. "I hope," wrote Congressman James A. Garfield in disgust, "we may not be compelled to push him four years more." [3] Even after the Chase boom failed, the Frémont movement collapsed, and the Republican convention renominated Lincoln, these Jacobins still hoped to replace him with a genuinely Radical candidate.

As to the outcome of this titanic struggle, which clearly prolonged the war by dividing the Northern people and by strengthening Southern resistance, historians differ. Some note that Lincoln in effect nullified the Radical program of confiscation, issued as weak and ineffectual a proclamation of emancipation as possible, sapped the powers of the Radical war governors, and broadened the conservative base of his support by converting the Republican into the Union party; he was thus, by 1865, in an admirable position to push for the adoption of his reconstruction program. Other writers argue that the Radicals were clearly winning. They secured the ousting of McClellan, the abolition of slavery, and the defeat of schemes to readmit the Southern states. Lincoln, declares Professor T. Harry Williams, "surrendered to the conquering Jacobins in every controversy before they could publicly inflict upon him a damaging reverse. Like the fair Lucretia threatened with ravishment, he averted his fate by instant compliance." [4]

So goes the cliché. There is a good deal to be said for it. Whatever its deficiencies, the picture of Lincoln battling the Radicals has been a useful corrective to the bland historiography of the post-Civil War Republican era, when Nicolay and Hay could write of Lincoln's renomination in 1864 as a certainty, since "the general drift of opinion was altogether in favor of intrusting to Mr. Lincoln the continuation of the work which he had thus far so well conducted." [5] The thesis has given artistic unity to some of the most important and useful books ever written about the Civil War. It is central, for example, to that greatest of Lincoln biographies, J. G. Randall's *Lincoln the President*, and it is basic to such admirable monographs as William B. Hesseltine's *Lincoln and the War Governors* and Professor Williams' *Lincoln and the Radicals*.

Further, one must note in fairness that this cliché is not the invention of these later historians. The terms "Radical" and "Conservative" were widely used during the Civil War years to characterize Republican factions. For example, Senator Orville H. Browning wrote in his diary of "These ultra, radical, unreasoning men who raised the insane cry of on to Richmond in July 1861, and have kept up a war on our generals ever since —who forced thro the confiscation bills, and extorted from the President the [emancipation] proclamation and lost him the confidence of the country"; they were, Browning held, Lincoln's "bitterest enemies, . . . doing all in their power to break him down." [6] Other Republicans were proud to be christened Radicals. Speaking of the President's revocation of General David Hunter's emancipation order in 1862, Senator James W. Grimes of Iowa wrote, "All the radical Republicans are indignant but me, and I am not, because I have expected it, and was ready for it." [7]

It should be added that, whatever the truth of the cliché of President versus Radicals, it does cast an important light upon Lincoln's own mind. Though the President was careful to avoid an open break with his critics and squelched a newspaper story which had him speaking of the "Jacobinism of Congress," [8] it is nevertheless clear that he often felt himself at loggerheads with Radical opponents. In unguarded moments he spoke of "the petulant and vicious fretfulness of many Radicals," [9] and he told Attorney-General Bates that some of their plots "were almost *fiendish*." [10] Doubtless the President got a great deal of satisfaction in thus personalizing the opposition to his administration.

II

For all its usefulness and general acceptance, the picture of Lincoln battling the Radicals may be less a photograph than a caricature. Historians are curiously imprecise in explaining just who these Radical opponents of Lincoln were. Virtually all agree that the group should include Charles Sumner, that classical ornament of the Republican party; dour, embittered Thaddeus Stevens; the ambitious, calculating Salmon P. Chase; and blunt Benjamin F. Wade. In addition, the names of Henry Winter Davis, Benjamin F. Butler, Wendell Phillips, Zachariah Chandler, and George W. Julian are usually mentioned. But beyond this nucleus, membership in the Radical club is vague. Does a figure like Lyman Trumbull belong? He participated in virtually all of the so-called anti-Lincoln maneuvers of the Radicals during the first three years of the war—only to emerge in 1865 as the chief senatorial defender of Lincoln's reconstruction program. What does one do about John A. Andrew and William Pitt Fessenden, both presumably harsh Radical opponents of Lincoln's who became important spokesmen for sectional reconciliation and for Lincolnian generosity after Appomattox? Even more difficult to classify is Andrew Johnson, who participated eagerly in the anti-Lincoln Committee on the Conduct of the War, only to become the pro-Lincoln military governor of Tennessee and Lincoln's hand-picked vice-presidential candidate in 1864.[11]

To identify the Conservative Republican opponents of these Radicals is even more puzzling. Since virtually all writers speak of the Radicals as a coterie or a cabal, the clear implication is that the Conservatives were in a majority. Yet when one begins to search he can find only William H. Seward, who was largely out of politics during the war years, and political ciphers like Gideon Welles and James Dixon. The principal Conservative Republican in Congress bore the revealing name of Doolittle.

Since there is difficulty in ascertaining just who the Radicals were, it is obviously not easy to learn what views they held in common. There was certainly no unity of Radical opinion before the presidential election of 1860, for that indubitable Radical, Charles Sumner, favored the nomination of Seward[12] while that equally Radical editor Horace Greeley spoke favorably of old-fogy Edward Bates.[13] Nor did Radical leaders agree upon policy in the secession crisis. Radicals Wade and Chandler welcomed a war,[14] but Radical Salmon P. Chase favored temporary secession, believing that the South, "after an unsatisfactory experiment of separation," would return chastened to the Union,[15] and Greeley, in one of his many passing moods, spoke of a permanent separation.[16]

To be sure, all Radicals were antislavery men—as, indeed, were most Northerners of all parties—but they differed as to how the South's peculiar institution should be eradicated. Thaddeus Stevens and Wendell Phillips argued that the United States Constitution was a proslavery document which forbade federal interference with slavery inside the Southern states; Chase and Sumner argued, to the contrary, that the Constitution was antislavery because it incorporated the principles of the Declaration of Independence. Once the war broke out, Greeley and Sumner urged President Lincoln to free all the slaves in order to crush the rebellion. "The heads of the hydra will be extirpated," Sumner said, "and the monster destroyed, never more to show itself." But the equally Radical Chase, on the other hand, favored a proclamation which would attack slavery "where it has done most mischief and where its extinction will do most good in weakening rebellion and incidentally otherwise in the extreme South," rather than a general emancipation.[17] Nor did Radicals agree on the future of the Negro at the end of the war. Sumner moved slowly and reluctantly toward enfranchising all the former slaves only when he found there was no chance of imposing a general educational test upon all Southern voters;[18] Chase boldly favored Negro suffrage in principle.[19] As to reconstruction policies as a whole, there were material differences between Sumner's "state suicide" theory and Stevens' "conquered province" idea[20]—and neither view was entirely acceptable to other leading Radicals.

Even more shaky is the customary generalization that the Radicals shared a plan to promote the manufacturing and banking interests of the Northeast. To be sure, most of them supported the tariff increases of the Civil War years, though Sumner had intellectual reservations about protection[21] and Greeley claimed that he wanted high tariffs as a step toward ultimate free trade.[22] Many Radicals, especially those who had once been Whigs, strongly favored government grants for internal improvements and of course supported the proposed transcontinental railroad, but Radical Senator Grimes called it "monstrous" to create a railroad monopoly, to which the United States government would give "such beneficent advantages, prerogatives, and privileges." [23] It should also be remembered that it was Radical Senator Sumner who introduced the first bill for the federal regulation of railroads ever proposed in Congress, a move in which Radical Horace Greeley backed him, but other Radicals killed his measure in committee.[24]

Financial questions exposed sharp differences among the Radicals. Secretary Chase's national banking bill, which is correctly viewed as a measure favoring the creditor interests of the Northeast, received the votes of most Radicals, but both Thaddeus Stevens and Grimes thought it a mistake.[25] Some of the Radicals abhorred inflation and urged a prompt return to specie payments, but Radicals Wade, Butler, and Stevens all championed greenback inflation.[26] Most Radicals—indeed, most congressmen—stood for the sanctity of private property, yet Stevens and Sumner proposed to create economic democracy in the conquered South by dividing plantations among the freedmen—a proposal that other Radicals condemned as "a piece of political vengeance wreaked without the intervention of courts of justice, in defiance of the forms of law and to the ruin of the innocent and helpless." [27]

This is not to argue that the Radicals shared no ideas. On most issues they saw eye to eye—but not merely with other

Radicals, but with Republicans of all persuasions. Too often it is forgotten that all Republicans disliked slavery and that virtually all realized from the beginning that war would put an end to it. Sumner's Radical view that the war offered the perfect opportunity for completing the antislavery crusade was shared by his Conservative rival, Charles Francis Adams, who declared flatly, "The slave question must be settled this time once for all." [28] Both opinions were mild in comparison with the plan of the extremely Conservative Orville H. Browning, who wanted to "subjugate the South, establish a black republic in lieu of the exterminated whites, and extend a protectorate over them while they raised our cotton." [29]

Too many historians have failed to look at the voting patterns of the Civil War Congresses. These show, not Republican factionalism but an extraordinary degree of Republican unanimity upon all measures designed to win the war, and especially upon all measures attacking slavery. The First Confiscation Act of 1861, often taken as the opening gun in the Radicals' war upon the South, passed the Senate without a division; in the House it received the support of 59 Republicans and was opposed by only 9.[30] The more stringent Second Confiscation Act of 1862, highly objectionable to President Lincoln, was backed by 82 Republicans in the House and was opposed by only 5, 4 of whom came from the Border States.[31] In December, 1862, 76 Republican congressmen endorsed a motion declaring the Emancipation Proclamation to be "warranted by the Constitution" and "well adapted to hasten the restoration of peace"; only 7, mostly from the Border States, opposed.[32] No Republican in either House or Senate opposed the Thirteenth Amendment, ending slavery throughout the land, when it came to a vote in 1864;[33] when it was once more brought before Congress in January, 1865, again every voting Republican in the House supported it.[34]

Even on the more controversial issues of reconstruction there was astonishing Republican unity. Only 6 Republicans in the House of Representatives voted against the Wade-Davis bill, designed to take the reconstruction process out of the hands of President Lincoln; 5 of these came from Border States. In the Senate 24 Republicans, including such alleged Conservatives as Doolittle and Henderson, supported the measure; none voted against it.[35] On the crucial proposal to admit Lincoln's reconstructed government of Arkansas, only 5 Republicans in the Senate backed the President; 20 voted to exclude the Arkansas senators.[36]

Similarly, the military views of the Radicals were shared by nearly all Republicans. Radical hostility to General McClellan is well known and elaborately documented, but equally authentic are Seward's protests against the general's "imbecility,"[37] Bates's complaints of his "criminal tardiness," "fatuous apathy," and "grotesque egotism,"[38] and Lincoln's own animadversions upon his slowness and his unwillingness to fight.[39]

Nor were the Radicals alone in deploring the weakness and incompetence of the Lincoln administration. It is instructive to select a few passages dealing with this issue from one of the most famous Civil War diaries. The Lincoln administration, complained the author, "has no system—no unity—no accountability—no subordination." The government was "lamentably deficient in the lack of unity and co-action." Lincoln had, "in fact, no *Cabinet*, and the show of Cabinet-councils is getting more and more, a mere show—Little matters or isolated propositions are sometimes talked over, but the great business of the country—questions of leading policy—are not mentioned." Lincoln, declared the diarist, was able to cope with "Neither great *principles* nor great *facts*." Indeed, the President, "an excellent man, and, in the main wise," simply lacked "*will* and *purpose*" and had "not *the power to command*." Consequently "bold and importunate men" were able to capitalize upon the President's "*amiable weakness*," and his administration ex-

hibited "shameful vaccilation [*sic*]." The author of these remarks was not Salmon P. Chase nor Adam Gurowski; it was the
extremely Conservative Edward Bates, Lincoln's own attorney-
general.[40]

Since most Republicans were dissatisfied with Lincoln's administration, most thought he should reconstitute his cabinet.
Radicals and Conservatives agreed upon this issue. In January,
1863, for example, Conservative David Davis of Illinois demanded "an instant reorganization of the Cabinet," so as to
make the government more efficient and popular.[41] More revealing of the complexity of Republican factionalism was the letter
written by the Conservative Montgomery Blair to Lincoln in
February, 1865, urging the President to drop the Conservative
Seward from the cabinet—and appoint as secretary of state the
Radical Sumner.[42] It is hardly surprising to find, upon restudy,
that the famous senatorial attempt of December, 1862, to force
the President to form a new cabinet was no Radical plot; it was
endorsed by all but two members of the Republican caucus and
the head of the senatorial committee of seven which confronted
the President was not Wade or Sumner but the Conservative
Jacob Collamer.[43]

It is quite true that many Radical Republicans did not think
highly of Lincoln as a man or as a president. Before painting
too dramatic a picture of their criticism, however, it must be
remembered that this was an age of uninhibited and articulate
individualism in American politics. Lincoln should not be singled
out as a special martyr. Republican attacks upon him were no
more shrill and unseemly than had been Democratic assaults
upon Presidents Pierce and Buchanan, and they were no more
vindictive than were subsequent Republican denunciations of
Presidents Johnson and Grant.

In discussing Radical opposition to Lincoln's renomination in
1864, one must keep in mind that most Republicans, including
the President himself, were dubious about his chances for re-

election. If Radical John A. Andrew wanted to persuade Lincoln to withdraw so that the Republicans could nominate another candidate, so did Conservative Thurlow Weed.[44] In the final count, of course, virtually all Radicals, and most Conservatives as well, voted for Lincoln rather than for McClellan.

III

THE CLICHÉ of Lincoln versus the Radicals, then, rests upon imprecise definition of terms and upon insufficient analysis of the evidence. It fails to define who the Radicals were; it fails to account for their very considerable differences of opinion; and it fails to recognize that most of their shared beliefs were also common to all Republicans.

Inevitably one is tempted to ask why such a shaky thesis should find support among distinguished historians noted for their careful scholarship. Their error, if it be one, clearly does not stem from shoddy research. Instead, one may suggest, the fault derives from what Oliver Wendell Holmes used to call an unstated major premise. Virtually all the writers who have developed this theme have agreed that Abraham Lincoln's program of conducting the war and winning the peace was sound, sensible, and statesmanlike. With this assumption, they have found it difficult to accept the fact that criticism of the Lincoln administration stemmed from widespread and realistic discontent with the policies of the government; instead, they have attributed anti-Lincoln sentiment to the activities of a little group of willful Radicals.

Whatever the truth of this interpretation, it shares the usual failing of historical hindsight; it does not take into account the feelings of the actual participants in the Civil War crisis. Instead of viewing the period retrospectively, from a vantage point where Lincoln's reputation is beyond historical assault, it might be helpful to reconstruct the situation as a public-spirited, informed Northerner would have been obliged to see it during the war years. Such a citizen when he read his daily paper would see little evidence of Lincolnian wisdom. Instead, his headlines told him that his government was corruptly and inefficiently managed and that it was an inept and disorganized bureaucracy.

At the head of that ineffective government he would see a well-meaning but incompetent President, who appeared to lack even political astuteness. Few contemporaries could discern much evidence of Lincoln's vaunted political sagacity. His proposal that all Northerners forget their political differences and form one giant Union party seemed unworkable and unrealistic; furthermore, it might seriously hinder the prosecution of the war.[45] Lincoln, we often forget, was to his contemporaries a chief executive who, even in wartime when public opinion was aroused and united, had to resort to arbitrary arrests, to suppression of newspapers, and even to outright deployment of troops during critical elections in order to retain his place.[46]

As for Lincoln's desire to keep the Civil War from becoming a social revolution, the best an informed Northern contemporary could say was that it might prevent the polarization of Union opinion into warring extremes. On the other hand, the President's moderation appeared to dampen the enthusiasm for the war, and, after all, it failed to produce the unity for which he sought. A genuinely antislavery man necessarily felt that Lincoln's policy of gradual emancipation, protracted if necessary to 1900, condemned three million Negro Americans to two more generations of cruel and intolerable servitude. When public opinion compelled the President to abandon these unworkable schemes, he resorted to an emancipation proclamation which managed to offend the abolitionists of the North without conciliating the reactionary racists. And, as so many contemporaries noted, the proclamation had the additional defect of being ineffective, because it applied only to slaves in territory controlled by the Confederates. Seward said that the proclamation did not free a single slave, and Lincoln himself had doubts of its legal validity.[47]

Nor was there much to be said in favor of Lincoln's military policy, designed to conduct the war without disturbing the Southern social system. Radicals and Conservatives agreed in deploring his retention of McClellan in command—an opinion in which most modern military historians concur.[48]

Nor could an informed Northerner see much promise in Lincoln's program for reconstruction, which later historians have so often extolled as a model of statesmanship. A great many congressmen were aware that the President was failing to take into account the inflamed state of passions, North and South, and that he was erroneously presupposing a reasonable, relaxed period of adjustment. It took no great foresight, either, to see that Lincoln was incorrectly assuming that the Southern whites, left to themselves with a minimum of federal guidance, would work out a program to safeguard the rights of the Negroes. To most Northerners, this was like asking the wolves to guarantee the rights of the sheep. Such doubts were, in fact, all too justified, for the reconstruction governments set up by the President did not secure basic justice to the freedmen. Not even presidential urging could persuade the restored government in Louisiana to grant a highly restricted vote to a small group of Negroes.[49] When continued by Andrew Johnson, these provisional governments showed their true temper by enacting the "Black Codes," which reduced the former slaves to virtual peonage.[50] Nor could a concerned Northerner accept the President's assurance that these governments in the conquered South were only tentative and provisional and that their acts were, in Lincoln's own phrase, as the egg to the fowl. As Charles Sumner remarked, out of crocodile eggs come only crocodiles.[51] The best a public-spirited Northerner could say for Lincoln's reconstruction policy was that, with his political pragmatism, the President refused to be committed inflexibly to any single plan[52] and that perhaps, with time, he might have come to modify his program.

It is not necessary for a historian to agree with these contemporary strictures upon Lincoln the President, but it is important to remember that he was, as J. G. Randall has reminded us, "The Unpopular Mr. Lincoln." Against such a background of uneasy distrust it is easier to understand that the opposition to Lincoln was not a plot by a little band of conspirators in his own party. Instead, virtually all Republicans, whether as Conservative as Thurlow Weed or as Radical as Thaddeus Stevens, were deploring what they considered Lincoln's genial incompetence, his amiable blundering, and his short-sighted want of planning.

IV

INSTEAD of the convention cliché of a benevolent Lincoln attacked by vindictive Radicals, then, the historian should substitute a complex picture of intraparty feuding, backbiting, and recrimination. The Republican party, it becomes clear, was not truly a national organization during the Civil War years but a coalition of state parties. In many instances these parties were rent by factionalism. The alignment of one faction behind the Lincoln administration and the sending of another into opposition was less a matter of "Conservative" versus "Radical" than of rivalry over power, position, and patronage. In Kansas, for example, the Republican party was distracted by the struggle between Senators S. C. Pomeroy and J. H. Lane.[53] There were no discernible ideological differences between the two men; both were equally vigorous in assailing Lincoln's war policies. But when Pomeroy attached himself to the political fortunes of Secretary Chase, Lane, to bolster his political position in Kansas—and to secure further federal patronage—promptly aligned himself behind the President. Similarly, Maryland was torn by a feud between the Republican Blair family and the Republican Henry Winter Davis.[54] At the outset of the war it was impossible to say which of these was Conservative and which Radical. But when Lincoln chose Montgomery Blair as his postmaster-general, Davis, who had himself desired a cabinet post, was left with no alternative but to assume a strong anti-administration position. In Massachusetts, no small part of Sumner's criticism of Lincoln's foreign policy stemmed from the appointment of his principal Republican enemy, Charles Francis Adams, as minister to Great Britain, an office which Sumner himself desired.

The complex story of Missouri Republican factionalism is most instructive upon this point. At first glance it would seem to reinforce the stereotype of a Conservative President opposed by his Radical foes, for Lincoln, at the advice of the Blairs and Bates, did generally give his support to the Conservative faction and the embittered Radicals sent the only anti-Lincoln delegation to the Baltimore convention in 1864.[55] But privately Lincoln made it clear that it was not ideology but personality which divided him from the Missouri Radicals. His critics, he told John Hay, were "the unhandiest devils in the world to deal with," but, he added, "after all their faces are set Zionwards." [56] "I know these Radical men have in them the stuff which must save the state and on which we must mainly rely," he continued. "They are absolutely uncorrosive by the virus of secession. It cannot touch or taint them. While the Conservatives, in casting about for votes to carry through their plans, are tempted to affiliate with those whose record is not clear. If one side *must* be crushed out & the other cherished there could be no doubt which side we would choose as fuller of hope for the future. We would have to side with the Radicals." [57]

These factional fights were not entirely aimless, however, for behind many of them lay the ancient rivalries between former Whigs and former Democrats. Though recent historians have minimized the significance of party differences in American history, it can be argued that Whigs and Democrats did disagree on such important matters as the powers of the president, the relative strength of the national and state governments, and the relation of the government to the economy. At any rate, it is certain that members of those parties thought they represented differing and opposing principles.[58] The party which elected Abraham Lincoln in 1860 was chiefly an amalgam of these old rival groups, and it was natural that these earlier antagonisms should continue into the war years. Behind the Blair-Davis feud in Maryland, for example, lay the genuine differences between Jacksonian Democrat and Clay Whig. In Illinois, Republicans of Democratic antecedents followed Lyman Trumbull, and those of Whig origins listened to his rival, David Davis.[59] In New York, the power and patronage given to the Whiggish Seward-Weed wing of the party alienated such former Democrats as William Cullen Bryant and Parke Godwin. It is at least suggestive that when former-Democrat Chase was attempting to replace Lincoln in 1864 he received his principal support from ex-Democrats now in the Republican party.

This Whig-Democratic tension within the Republican party was especially apparent when the question of restoring the Southern states to the Union was under discussion. The essential problem of reconstruction was to locate dependable Unionists within the South, to whom the future of that section could be safely entrusted. Republicans of Whig origins naturally tended to think of the Southern planters and merchants with whom they had once been allied in the old Whig party. Lincoln's own reconstruction measures were based upon the assumption that this Southern upper class had been coerced into secession and upon the belief that, if encouraged, they would again give conservative leadership to their section. Perhaps the President envisaged the kind of revival of Whiggery, North and South, which was actually attempted in the 1876–77 crisis over the election of Rutherford B. Hayes.[60] Former Democrats in the Republican party, on the other hand, thought of the great Whig planters as conspirators who had taken their states into secession in order to preserve slavery and consequently looked for real Unionism among their former Democratic political allies, the small farmers of the South. Andrew Johnson's program of excluding wealthy Southerners from leadership in the reconstruction process was a reflection of his Democratic antecedents. Only those thoroughly embittered Republicans like Stevens and Sumner, who saw no Unionism anywhere in the white population of the South, turned to the Negro as the guarantor of Northern victory.

This intricate pattern of intraparty Republican rivalries, personal, political, and ideological, offers a truer picture of Civil War politics than our present oversimplifications about Lincoln versus the Radicals. Doubtless such a complicated story will not secure easy popular acceptance, for, as T. S. Eliot reminds us, "Human kind cannot bear very much reality." It is, however, the function of the historian to recreate the past in all its rich complexity, and not to reiterate outworn clichés.

NOTES

1. The most scholarly, complete, and closely reasoned statement of this thesis is T. Harry Williams, *Lincoln and the Radicals* (Madison, 1941); quotations in the next two paragraphs are taken from pp. 5–9 of this source. I raised some questions about this interpretation in "The Radicals and Lincoln," in my *Lincoln Reconsidered: Essays on the Civil War Era* (New York, 1956), pp. 103–127. As is indicated by Professor Williams' contribution to the present volume—a paper which, of course, I did not see until my own had been completed—he appears to have accepted the more important of my criticisms, and our points of view are not now very different. Though Professor Williams himself no longer stresses the antagonism between Lincoln and the Radicals, his earlier work remains influential, and it seems fair to quote it as still the best formulation of the viewpoint with which I disagree.

2. Willard H. Smith, *Schuyler Colfax: The Changing Fortunes of a Political Idol* ("Indiana Historical Collections," Vol. XXXIII; Indianapolis, 1952), pp. 177–178.

3. Theodore Clarke Smith, *The Life and Letters of James Abram Garfield* (New Haven, 1925), I, 375.

4. Williams, p. 18.

5. John G. Nicolay and John Hay, *Abraham Lincoln: A History* (New York, 1890), VIII, 309.

6. Theodore Calvin Pease and James G. Randall, eds., *The Diary of Orville Hickman Browning* ("Collections of the Illinois State Historical Library," Vol. XX; Springfield, 1925), I, 598.

7. William Salter, *The Life of James W. Grimes* (New York, 1876), p. 196.

8. Roy P. Basler and others, eds., *The Collected Works of Abraham Lincoln* (New Brunswick, 1953), VIII, 39–40.

9. Nicolay and Hay, IX, 100.

10. Howard K. Beale, ed., *The Diary of Edward Bates, 1859–1866* (Washington, 1933), p. 333.

11. There is, of course, a dispute as to Lincoln's part in the selection of Johnson, but for a careful evaluation of the evidence see J. G. Randall and Richard N. Current, *Lincoln the President: The Last Full Measure* (New York, 1955), pp. 130–134.

12. David Donald, *Charles Sumner and the Coming of the Civil War* (New York, 1960), p. 531.

13. Glyndon G. Van Deusen, *Horace Greeley: Nineteenth Century Crusader* (Philadelphia, 1953), pp. 241–243.

14. *Congressional Globe,* 36 Cong., 2 sess., pp. 100–103; The Detroit Post and Tribune, *Zachariah Chandler: An Outline Sketch of His Life and Public Services* (Detroit, 1880), p. 190.

15. Robert Bruce Warden, *An Account of the Private Life and Public Services of Salmon Portland Chase* (Cincinnati, 1874), p. 371.

16. David M. Potter, "Horace Greeley and Peaceable Secession," *Journal of Southern History,* VII (1941), 145–159.

17. For a careful study of Radical opinion on this topic see W. David Wells, "The Radical Republicans in the Civil War Era" (unpublished senior thesis, Department of History, Princeton University, 1961), Chap. II.

18. Robert Cruden, *James Ford Rhodes: The Man, the Historian, and His Work* (Cleveland, 1961), p. 76.

19. S. P. Chase to Abraham Lincoln, Baltimore, April 11, 1865, in Robert Todd Lincoln Collection (Library of Congress).

20. Eric L. McKitrick, *Andrew Johnson and Reconstruction* (Chicago, 1961), pp. 99–101, 110–113.

21. Edward L. Pierce, *Memoir and Letters of Charles Sumner* (Boston, 1893), IV, 24–25.

22. *New York Daily Tribune,* June 23, 1861, quoted in Wells, p. 94.

23. Salter, p. 254.

24. Charles Sumner, *The Works of Charles Sumner* (Boston, 1875), IX, 237–265; David F. Trask, "Charles Sumner and the New Jersey Railroad Monopoly during the Civil War," *Proceedings of the New Jersey Historical Society,* LXXV (Oct., 1957), 259–275.

25. Richard Nelson Current, *Old Thad Stevens* (Madison, 1942), p. 246; Salter, pp. 214–215.

26. Irwin F. Unger, "Men, Money, and Politics: The Specie Resumption Issue, 1865–1879" (unpublished Ph.D. dissertation, Department of History, Columbia University, 1958), *passim.*

27. *The Nation* (New York), IV (May 16, 1867), 394–395.

28. Williams, p. 10.

29. John Hay, Diary, May 7, 1861, photostat of MS (Massachusetts Historical Society).

30. Edward McPherson, ed., *The Political History of the United States of America, during the Great Rebellion* (3rd ed.; Washington, 1876), pp. 195–196. The nine were not, in fact, all Republicans; McPherson loosely grouped together all "Unionists" in this Congress.

31. *Ibid.,* p. 197.

32. *Ibid.,* p. 229.

33. *Ibid.,* p. 258.

34. *Ibid.,* p. 590.

35. *Ibid.,* pp. 317–318.

36. *Ibid.,* p. 321.

37. Hay, Diary (MS), undated entry written during early months of 1862.

38. Donald, *Lincoln Reconsidered,* p. 112.

39. T. Harry Williams, *Lincoln and His Generals* (New York, 1952), pp. 177–178.

40. Beale, pp. 196, 220, 280, 283, 302, 422.

41. Pease and Randall, I, 616.

42. Nicolay and Hay, IX, 349.

43. Donald, *Lincoln Reconsidered,* pp. 113–114.

44. Thurlow Weed to W. H. Seward, Aug. 10, 1864, and Weed to F. W. Seward, Aug. 26, 1864, Seward MSS (University of Rochester).

45. David M. Potter, "Jefferson Davis and the Political Factors in Confederate Defeat," in David Donald (ed.), *Why the North Won the Civil War* (Baton Rouge, 1960), pp. 112–114.

46. William B. Hesseltine, *Lincoln and the War Governors* (New York, 1948) is one of the few studies which sufficiently emphasizes such matters.

47. On the ineffectiveness of the proclamations, see J. G. Randall, *Lincoln and the South* (Baton Rouge, 1946), pp. 98–101.

48. The fullest statement of the anti-McClellan position is Kenneth P. Williams, *Lincoln Finds a General* (5 vols.; New York, 1949–1959). See also T. Harry Williams, *Lincoln and His Generals*—which does a great deal to refute Professor Williams' earlier argument in *Lincoln and the Radicals.* One of the few present-day military historians to defend McClellan is Warren W. Hassler, Jr., in *General George B. McClellan: Shield of the Union* (Baton Rouge, 1957). In *Lincoln the President* J. G. Randall also presented a strong brief for McClellan, but he made no claim to be a military expert.

49. John Rose Ficklen, *History of Reconstruction in Louisiana (through 1868)* (Baltimore, 1910), pp. 63–64.

50. J. G. Randall and David Donald, *The Civil War and Reconstruction* (2nd ed.; Boston, 1961), pp. 571–574.

51. Sumner, X, 44.

52. William B. Hesseltine, *Lincoln's Plan of Reconstruction* (Tuscaloosa, 1960), *passim*.

53. Harry J. Carman and Reinhard H. Luthin, *Lincoln and the Patronage* (New York, 1943), pp. 228–229.

54. Reinhard H. Luthin, "A Discordant Chapter in Lincoln's Administration: The Davis-Blair Controversy," *Maryland Magazine of History,* XXXIX (1944), 25–48.

55. The fullest account of these developments is William E. Parrish, *Turbulent Partnership: Missouri and the Union, 1861–1865* (Columbia, Missouri, 1963).

56. Hay, Diary (MS), Oct. 28 [1863].

57. *Ibid.,* Dec. 10, 1863.

58. David Donald, "Abraham Lincoln: Whig in the White House," in Norman A. Graebner (ed.), *The Enduring Lincoln* (Urbana, 1959), pp. 55–66.

59. Willard King, *Lincoln's Manager: David Davis* (Cambridge, 1960), pp. 182, 200–201.

60. I am indebted to Professor Kenneth M. Stampp, of the University of California, for this suggestion. The importance of the old Whigs in the Hayes-Tilden election has been documented by C. Vann Woodward in *Reunion and Reaction: The Compromise of 1877 and the End of Reconstruction* (Boston, 1951).

Lincoln and the Radicals: An Essay in Civil War History and Historiography

by T. Harry Williams

THE POLITICIANS were drifting into Washington for the opening of the second session of the thirty-seventh Congress, and Joshua F. Speed, Lincoln's friend, watching and weighing what he saw and heard in those early winter days of 1861, was apprehensive for the President and for what Speed conceived to be the President's policy. "I can see that Lincoln is going to have trouble with the fiery element of his own party," Speed advised a man who was, like himself, a border-state Unionist. Shortly Speed had more exact and more ominous information for his colleague: "I am fully persuaded that there is mischief brewing here; a large and powerful party of the ultra men is being formed to make war upon the President and upon his conservative policy." [1] The ultra men were, indeed, incensed at Lincoln, and they did organize for action against him. They called themselves the Radicals, and history knows them by that name, or as the Radical Republicans. They may or may not have made war on Lincoln—historians, who are marvelously talented at giving different meanings to the same phrase, differ on this issue—but at the very least they made him deep and constant trouble in the years ahead. In 1864 many of them were prepared, as Lincoln well knew, to prevent his renomination as the Republican standard-bearer. "He is fully apprehensive of the schemes of the Radical leaders," recorded Attorney General Edward Bates in his diary. "He is also fully aware that they would strike him at once, if they durst; but they fear that the blow would be ineffectual, and so, they would fall under his power, as beaten enemies." [2]

Men like Speed and Bates considered themselves to be Conservative Republicans, and if they sometimes thought that Abraham Lincoln was not always as conservative as he should be they nevertheless counted him on their side. So also did the Radicals rank him, and they were certain that they knew what conservatism was and they were contemptuous of both its practices and its practitioners, whether they were Lincoln or lesser men. Speaking of Senator William P. Fessenden, who moved among the Radicals without being completely one of them, Thaddeus Stevens sneered: "He has too much of the vile ingredient, called conservatism, which is worse than secessionism." [3] A Radical newspaper derided the leadership of its own party as "this albino administration, and its diluted spawn of pink eyed patriots—this limp result of the feeble embrace of half-furnished conservatives and limited emancipators." [4] The Radicals were also certain that they would defeat the Conservatives, and they knew why they would win—it was because they comprehended the right doctrine, because they realized the divine purpose, because they were the appointed instruments to eradicate evil. In 1865, at the moment of victory, Senator "Bluff Ben" Wade exultingly described for the Senate how belief in principle had enabled the Radicals to lay conservatism in the dust. Wade, who considered Lincoln or anybody to the right of himself as a conservative, explained that the Conservatives, once so powerful, had lost out because they were without principle, and being such, they made the fatal error of opposing the destruction of the slavery monster. "But where are you now," he asked, "ye conservatives, that then stood with your heads so high? The radicals have their feet upon your necks, and they are determined that their feet shall rest on the neck of the monster until he breathes his last." [5]

There were, then, in the Republican party during the Civil War men and factions that called themselves Radicals and Conservatives, and they spoke of their beliefs as entities that could be identified and segregated one from the other. Their sense or system of dichotomy has passed into the historical writing about the war. The conflict between the Radicals and the Conservatives, revolving around the wartime disposal to be made of slavery, looms large in all the books, and has been until recently a staple article in all analyses of Northern and Republican politics. But now it has been challenged by some scholars and most notably by Professor David Donald, whose original insights have done so much to illumine our understanding of the broader nature of the war. In a stimulating essay, "The Radicals and Lincoln," [6] Professor Donald suggests that we discard altogether the Radical-Conservative polarism. His argument, if I do it justice, runs as follows. Historians have made the Radicals the villains of an illusory struggle. Any president is bound to disappoint most of the people who voted for him, even as many as nine-tenths of them; so Lincoln disappointed his followers, most of whom, regardless of their factional persuasion, viewed him as incompetent or imperfect; Lincoln, like every president, was the center of a tug for power between various groups in his party; he worked with these factions, including the Radicals, and not against them; and in the final analysis Lincoln has no serious differences with the Radicals, who were not a cohesive faction during the war and did not become one until Reconstruction. In short, Mr. Donald seems to be telling us that what we have supposed was an important and unique conflict was only an expression of the normal workings of American politics and that such contests characterize all administrations. Having disposed of the Civil War Radicals, Mr. Donald apparently is content to rest, but others want to push his thesis toward new frontiers. Professor Eric McKitrick, in a recent study of Reconstruction, states that the Radicals were not a particularly cohesive or effective faction even in the years after the war and that they did not control the process of reconstruction. [7] Obviously we are moving toward a new interpretation of the whole Civil War era which will run thus: There were no Radicals and besides they weren't very radical.

This latest view of the Radicals, this revision of revisionism, we may say, reflects in part one of the most settled convictions of historians—that they know more about what the people of a particular time were up to than the people concerned. But in larger measure it is the expression of something more important, of a new style or doctrine in historical thought. In recent years we have been subjected in the literature to what has been called the history of consensus and consent. Influenced by both the insecurities and the conservatism of our age, historians have sought for security and unity in the American past. They have depicted an America which has never been beset by serious differences or divisions, one in which all parties and factions have worked toward essentially the same objectives. The interpretive thrust of the new persuasion is seen most plainly in works treating the Revolutionary period and the Populist movement, but it has affected viewpoints in all areas of our history. It speaks in the Civil War era in the voices of Professors Donald, McKitrick, and others, and here it promises, Civil War historians being notoriously eager and able to bay after a fresh scent, to wax louder in the years ahead. There are, however, signs of a reaction against the whole concept of consensus history, and we may be about to experience one of those examinations of contrasting views that impel introspection and clarify the meaning of history. At this budding point in Civil War historiography, when new interpretations that have not entirely crystallized meet old ones that may need modification, it would seem essential to reconsider the issue most in dispute. The question at hand might be phrased: Shall we keep the Radicals?

At the very beginning it is proper to say that whether Professor Donald is right or wrong in his analysis of Northern politics he has performed a needed service by clearing away some confusing underbrush. Previous historians have exaggerated the congruity of the Radicals and the sharpness of their differences with the Conservatives. And he supplies a helpful corrective to the accepted picture with his reminder that a degree of conflict is inherent in the operation of any of our parties. But he errs, it seems to me, on a number of points. For one, he attempts to write off differences of opinion as inconsequential by citing friendly surface manifestations between Lincoln and certain Radicals, notably Charles Sumner, although it is a familiar fact in politics that men with divergent opinions will nearly always keep up some kind of personal relationship; and for another, he conveys a wrong impression by stating that as many Conservatives as Radicals opposed Lincoln, giving as his examples men like Horatio Seymour, Reverdy Johnson, and O. H. Browning, who were really Democrats or political mavericks. The most serious flaw in his case, however, and it would seem a fatal one, is the assumption that the years between 1861 and 1865 represent a normal political situation marked by normal political reactions. It was not a normal situation because a war, a civil and a modern war, was being fought, and great wars have a way of overriding normality. It was not a normal condition because the paramount divisive issue of the war, as of the decade before, was slavery, an abnormal issue, the only issue in our history that defied the usual methods of political settlement, the only one that eventuated in a resort to force. Slavery was the kind of question that excited violent controversy even among people who were in general agreement as to its ultimate disposal. Finally, Professor Donald neglects, as have all of us who have written on the subject, to define who and what the Radicals were. We very much need a structure or pattern of Radicalism. This paper will attempt some tentative suggestions as to what that structure might be.

Any analysis of the Radicals must, of course, begin with some consideration of the Republican party, for the Radicals have to be related to other elements in the organization and to the organization as a whole. The Republican party was, perhaps because of its youth, a remarkably homogeneous and tenacious assemblage. Agglomerate in make-up, like all our major parties, it nevertheless displayed a fairly consistent purpose in moving toward its economic and political objectives. Its cohesiveness and cunning in the economic area have been exaggerated by historians, but still it was in substantial accord on vital legislation; certainly it was not rent by any serious economic differences, and those that arose were susceptible of ready adjustment. Like all parties, it had a strong institutional urge to survive, to grasp and hold the power and patronage that meant survival, and this quality has perhaps not been sufficiently noted by historians. Because it was new to the ways of office, it was especially avid to retain the rewards of office, and this desire invested it with a rare capacity to sustain internal differences and absorb them. The Republican factions could dispute constantly and violently among themselves until a crisis, like the election of 1864, threatened displacement. Then they quickly closed ranks—until the crisis had passed.

Only one serious divisive issue agitated the party, but this issue, because of its unique nature and because it tended to pull other issues into its orbit, was of overruling importance. The question was, of course, slavery, or more accurately, the policy to be adopted toward slavery during the war. All factions of the party were in one degree or another opposed to the peculiar institution and committed to its extinction. But they differed as to when and how it should be extinguished. To borrow European terms, on the slavery problem there was a right, a center, and a left faction. The right was made up mainly of border-state Unionists, such as Speed, Bates, and Montgomery Blair, who were antislavery more in theory than in fact, who were more content to talk against slavery than to act against it, and who hoped its ultimate extinction would come by state action and would be fairly ultimate. The center included the men whom we call, and who called themselves, the Conservative Republicans. Before the war they had advocated some plan to bring about the eventual and gradual disappearance of slavery, their favorite device being to prevent it from expanding to the territories and thus causing it to wither on the vine and die. Once the war started they were willing to hasten its demise; they thought that a plan should be devised during the war to accomplish the destruction of slavery *after* the war, preferably by a scheme of compensated emancipation. It was "the calm, deliberate opinion of that great conservative class," said Senator James Dixon, that slavery must go, but it should go out with order and proper ritual. The mood of the conservative approach was suggested by one journalist: "Slavery has been the cause of enormous wrongs, but it must not, therefore, be stricken in passionate revenge." [8] The left comprised the Radicals, who became during the war the dominant faction. The Radicals were more committed to the destruction of slavery than any of the other factions, and they were determined to use the war as an opportunity to strike it down. Put simply and baldly, their program was to destroy slavery as part of the war process, to destroy it suddenly and, if necessary, violently, to destroy it, if not in revenge, with passion.

All factions of the Republican party were united, then, on certain objectives. They were for the Union, they were for the war to preserve it, and they were antislavery. Only on the issue of how to proceed against slavery during the war did they divide seriously and significantly, and this division appeared, as Joshua Speed and others saw it would, almost immediately after the conflict began. Lincoln too saw the issue emerging, and he knew what it portended. As if sensing the program the Radicals would soon develop, the President, in his message to Congress of December, 1861, delineated what measures against slavery should not be executed. "In considering the policy to be adopted for suppressing the insurrection," he said, "I have been anxious and careful that the inevitable conflict for this purpose shall not degenerate into a violent and remorseless revolutionary struggle. . . . We should not be in haste to determine that radical and extreme measures, which may reach the loyal as well as the disloyal, are indispensable." Interestingly enough, when toward the end of the war George W. Julian described how the Radicals had wrenched control from the administration and imposed their own policy toward slavery, he used almost exactly Lincoln's own words to characterize the Radical procedure. From the beginning of the war the Radicals had, Julian explained, "persistently urged a vigorous policy, suited to remorseless and revolutionary violence, till the Government felt constrained to embrace it." [9] Politicians often indulge in an exaggerated and extreme rhetoric that makes them seem more agitated than they really are. But even allowing for this habit, it is evident that Lincoln and Julian, both of whom, incidentally, were more precise in language than most of their type, were talking about something that was very real and very vital to them. "Remorseless and revolutionary violence"—these are not the kind of terms customarily employed by politicians to characterize the program of other politicians, especially those of the same party; and these are not the kind of labels that American politicians ordinarily accept, let alone boast of wearing. We are dealing here, it is emphasized again, with something decidedly out of the ordinary in politics. The Civil War is the only episode in our history, or the only important episode, when men have insisted on the total or absolute solution to a problem, and in the North the Radicals were the men with the final solution. The divisive issue in the Republican party was, therefore, veritable, concrete, substantial, and, above all, abnormal to the political process.

In attempting to structure the Radicals, it is necessary at the start to discard any modern concepts of radicalism, notably those related to an economic basis. The Radicals and other Republicans may have had their differences on particular issues, but essentially their economic beliefs were fairly conventional.[10] Nor were the Radicals radical in the European sense of wanting to make over all at once all of society. But they were radical, as they realized and, indeed, proudly proclaimed, in one area of thought and action and on one issue. The area might be narrow but it contained most of the social tensions then occupying the American people, and the issue might be solitary but at the time it overrode all others. The Radicals were real radicals in that they wanted to accomplish a great change in society, or in one part of it, namely, to destroy slavery and to punish those who supported slavery. They proposed to effect this change suddenly and without much regard for the opinions of those who opposed them, and without much thought of the problems that such a change might bring, especially to the people most concerned, those in the South. They were, then, radical and even revolutionary in attitude and temperament; and if not all Radicals subscribed in toto to every aspect of the attitude or recognized every action required by it, they are still identifiable as a faction. If they were not radical in the accepted or European sense, they are yet the closest approach to a real radical group we have had in this country.

The broadest characterization to be made of the Radicals, the one that encompasses practically all their qualities, is that they were doctrinaire and dogmatic. They possessed truth and justice and they had the total solution; they were men of principle and they were prepared to enforce their principles. "The radical men are the men of principle," Ben Wade boasted; "they are the men who feel what they contend for. They are not your slippery politicians who can jigger this way or that, or construe a thing any way to suit the present occasion. They are the men who go deeply down for principle and are not to be detached by any of your higgling. The sternness of their principle has revolutionized this whole continent." [11] In short, the Radicals were not pragmatic or empiric; and not being so, they were not typical or normal American politicians. They could not conceive that sometimes the imposition of right principles produces bad results, they could not credit that sometimes the removal of an evil may cause greater evils; they were so sure of their motives that they did not have to consider results. The rightness of their cause is not at stake, is not perhaps the kind of subject on which the historian should pronounce. Whatever the case, few would deny that the antislavery crusade had about it elements that were grandly righteous. But it was the kind of righteousness that reckoned little of consequence, especially the consequence to others.

Essentially the conflict in the Republican ranks was over how the problem of slavery should be approached, on a basis of principle or pragmatism. This is not to say that all Conservatives were pragmatic. Some were, in their own way, quite as doctrinaire as were most Radicals, but many were not; and the great Conservative and the great opponent of radicalism was the supreme pragmatist in our history. And it was precisely because he was what he was that the Radicals scorned and despised Abraham Lincoln. Professor Donald makes the point that many Republicans, Radicals and Conservatives alike, considered Lincoln to be indecisive and incompetent and said so, and he further observes that such personal denunciations of a president are heard in every administration. There is perception in this and also a lack of it. Historians will, of course, give different readings to the same documents, but it would seem that the personal criticism of Lincoln emanating from the Radicals was of a different order from that coming from other Republicans, being particularly savage and venomous. At any rate, we know that Lincoln was deeply pained by the tone of the Radical blasts, notably by the Wade-Davis Manifesto, and that he once spoke sadly of the "petulant and vicious fretfulness" displayed by most Radicals.[12]

But the Radicals went beyond mere evaluations of Lincoln as an executive or administrator. In their lexicon the theme was that the President was a man without principle or doctrine. He had no antislavery instincts, no crusading zeal to eradicate evil, no blueprint for reform, no grasp of immutable truth. Wendell Phillips, on the eve of the election of 1864, expressed exactly the Radical summation of Lincoln. The note struck by Phillips was not that Lincoln was incompetent or even bad but that being without dogma he was simply nothing. The administration had tried "many times," Phillips observed, to resist "the Revolution" embodied in radicalism but had been overborne by it. And if Lincoln was re-elected the administration would continue to resist; at the least, Lincoln, because he could not realize the importance of principle, would do nothing to assist the Revolution. The Radicals did indeed think that Lincoln was deficient, but not so much as a political operator as a moral leader, and it was primarily for this reason that they wanted to discard him in 1864. James A. Garfield stated revealingly the objections of the Radicals to a further tenure for Lincoln: "I hope we may not be compelled to push him four years more." [13] Running all through the Radical literature on Lincoln is a suggestion of condescension, the condescension of the ideologue for the pragmatist, of the generalist for the particularist. Because the President had no firmly based beliefs, charged Joshua R. Giddings, the party had been forced to abandon its fundamental beliefs. "We are to go into the next Presidential election without doctrines, principles, or character," Giddings wailed, and added contemptuously: "But to make the union and the support of the administration the test questions." Casting up at the end of the war the reasons for the triumph of the Union, L. Maria Child recalled the "want of moral grandeur" in the government during the first years of the war and the consequent failure of Northern arms. But then Radical counsels had come to prevail and immediately things changed: great ideas and great principles were installed and victory had naturally followed. Simple Lincoln had not understood that victory depended on the right doctrine, but he had gone along with the men who did. How fortunate it was after all, Miss Child patronized, that he had been a man who was willing to grow.[14]

The ardent feminine Radical was certain that the hearts of the soldiers had been sad and cold until the correct dogma had been instituted, whereupon they had become irresistible. But in the early stages of the war many Radicals, while they hoped the men in uniform would think right, did not wish them to become too victorious too soon. Rather, they were willing that the armies should fight on indefinitely, until the voters at home were persuaded to the Radical program; and if reverses in the field were necessary to effect this conversion the Radicals were quite content to have the soldiers suffer the reverses. This is not to say that the Radicals wanted the armies or the war to fail. But certainly many of them, in their devotion to doctrine, were prepared to prolong the struggle until their objectives were accomplished. "If it continues thirty years and bankrupts the whole nation," cried Ben Wade, "I hope to God there will be no peace until we can say there is not a slave in this land."[15] The speeches and writings of Radicals of all sizes are crammed with affirmations that defeat will be good for the popular soul, that penance and punishment must precede redemption. Wendell Phillips intoned: "God grant us so many reverses that the government may learn its duty; God grant us the war may never end till it leaves us on the solid granite of impartial liberty and justice."[16] And from that most doctrinaire of all Radicals, Charles Sumner, came this: "We are too victorious; I fear more from our victories than from our defeats. . . . The God of battles seems latterly to smile upon us. I am content that he should not smile too much. . . . There must be more delay and more suffering,—yet another 'plague' before all will agree to 'let my people go': and the war cannot, must not, end till then."[17] It is contended that such statements do not represent the normal sentiments of politicians discussing normal political issues. They are not oratory but theology. Whatever they reflect of the sincerity and sense of justice of the speakers, they reveal that determination in radicalism and abolitionism to remove evil regardless of who suffered, the sinners in the South and even the drafted instruments who were, at the right time, to crush the sinners. These are the implacable declarations of men who had the absolute solution and who would insist on that solution regardless of consequence. The pragmatist in the White House could not have spoken in such a spirit, nor would he, if he could help it, accept the solution.

As a part of the solution, the Radicals proposed to make over the social structure of the South, to make it over to accord with the dictates of moral theory. This determination is one of the most significant manifestations of their doctrinaire zeal. "The whole social system of the Gulf States is to be taken to pieces," exulted Phillips; "every bit of it." Thaddeus Stevens hoped for the same result, but he was skeptical that it could be achieved. "Whether we shall find anybody with a sufficient grasp of mind and sufficient moral courage, to treat this as a radical revolution, and remodel our institutions, I doubt," Stevens wrote. "It would involve the desolation of the South as well as emancipation; and a repeopling of half the continent. This ought to be done but it startles most men." [18] Not only would the Radicals reconstruct the society of a part of the country, but in the process of removing an evil that could not be abided they would punish the people responsible for the evil, punish them not reluctantly or with stern love but with a kind of ecstasy that went with the joy of doing God's will, with a zeal that became men charged with constituting a society that glorified their Creator. The punishment of slaveholders is an element that bulks large in Radical thought. It deserves more attention than it has received from historians as another key to the Radical psychology and as an indicator of the sweep of the Radical program. The Radicals proposed penalties that were not only stringent but remarkably durable.

From the Radical chorus on what should be done to the South a few voices are extracted. Owen Lovejoy: "If there is no other way to quell this rebellion, we will make a solitude, and call it peace." Zachariah Chandler: "A rebel has sacrificed all his rights. He has no right to life, liberty, property, or the pursuit of happiness. Everything you give him, even life itself, is a boon which he has forfeited." [19] Thaddeus Stevens: "Abolition—yes! abolish everything on the face of the earth but this Union; free every slave—slay every traitor—burn every Rebel mansion, if these things be necessary to preserve this temple of freedom to the world and to our posterity." Henry Wilson: "Sir, it seems to me that our duty is as clear as the track of the sun across the heavens, and that duty is before the adjournment of this Congress to lay low in the dust under our feet, so that iron heels will rest upon it, this great rebel, this giant criminal, this guilty murderer, that is warring upon the existence of this country." [20]

Again it is submitted that statements such as these are more than the rhetorical mouthings common to politicians, more than the customary commentaries on normal political issues. These are the expressions of abstract reformers who were so certain of their motives that they did not have to consider the results of their course, who were so convinced of their righteousness that they wanted to punish the sinners as well as the sin. One may readily concede that the antislavery cause was a noble endeavor and yet at the same time note, as Lincoln noted, that it had its darker and socially mischievous side. For the Radicals came and, being what they were, came soon to demand the very policy Lincoln had warned against when he begged his party not to resort to a "violent and remorseless revolutionary struggle." Historians have talked much about the deep-laid plans of the Radicals to solidify and expand their dominance in the years after the war. The recent revisionists have questioned this thesis, doubting that the Radicals saw that far ahead, and they are in part right. Indeed, on one count the opposite of the conventional view would seem to be true—that in their terrible certainty and zeal the Radicals did not look far enough into the future. Intent on removing a sin, they did not consider, as did the pragmatic Lincoln, that the sinners would have to be lived with after the war. They were for the Union but in it they would make no viable place for the defeated side. Perhaps the real criticism of the Radicals should be not that they planned too well but too little.

The Radicals not only spoke a revolutionary vocabulary, they employed on occasion revolutionary techniques. Somewhere along the line, probably in the long frustrating struggle against slavery, many of them had acquired revolutionary temperaments. To achieve their objectives or just to snap the unbearable tension of being unable to lay hands on evil, that is, slavery, they were willing to use short cuts, to skirt around the edges, to play loosely with accepted procedures; they talked openly of the end justifying the means; they were ruthlessly determined to accomplish their end because it was both theirs and right. We see one aspect of this psychology, and again the constant commitment to doctrine, in the insistent Radical demand that the management of the war, in its civilian and military branches, be entrusted exclusively to Radical antislavery men, to men who, in Radical terminology, had their hearts in the struggle. It may be said by some that the Radicals were only trying in the normal fashion of politicians to get their hands on some patronage. But surely any reading of the documents will demonstrate that this was more than just a grab for jobs. These dedicated doctrinaires intended if they could to proscribe from the government and the armies every individual who did not agree with them completely. The expressions of Radical opinion on this goal are too plentiful and too plain to admit of much doubt. Over and over they say that the President who did not know doctrine must be surrounded in his cabinet by men of doctrine, that the armies must be led by "generals of ideas" who were swayed by "the great invisible forces," that the imposition of a Radical policy on the administration would be barren unless it was administered by Radical men.[21]

The Radicals displayed their revolutionary spirit on many occasions and in several areas of government and politics. One of the most sensational manifestations was their attempt in 1864, first, to prevent Lincoln's renomination by the Republicans, and after that failed, to force his withdrawal as the party's candidate. The episode is a rare case of political behaviorism. In our system the party in power almost has to go into a presidential election with the man who has been president. If he wants the nomination, the party is constrained to give it to him, for to repudiate the man is to repudiate the party's record, and this is a party confession of failure. The business is so risky that it has rarely been tried. This rule of politics was not as well established in the nineteenth century as it later became but it was apparent then and should have been apparent to the Radicals in a wartime election. The most unique feature of the affair was the effort of some Radical leaders to force Lincoln off the ticket in the late summer and substitute for him a candidate named by the Republican National Committee.

In 1864 the Radicals wanted to deny Lincoln the nomination, partly because they thought he did not appreciate principle, partly because, in Garfield's words, they did not want to have to push him four years more, and partly because they felt they could not trust him to deal with the emerging problem of reconstruction. "He is hardly the man to handle the country, while its heart is overgenerous with reconstituted peace, so that due guarantees may be exacted from its enemies," observed a Radical editor.[22] As it turned out, the Radicals could not effect either of their objectives. They were unable to prevent Lincoln's nomination and they were unable to force him to yield up the nomination after he had won it. The reasons for their discomfiture were many and complex. Lincoln's popularity with the people and the politicians was too great to be disregarded. Many Republican leaders, including some Radicals, feared a disrupting fight in the party that might lead to a Democratic victory. And as bad as Lincoln was, he was infinitely better than any Democrat.[23]

It is true, as Professor Donald has reminded us, that many Republicans of all stripes were dubious about Lincoln's candidacy. But the Radicals were the core of the opposition to him, the men who organized to act against him, and whereas other Republicans diverged from Lincoln for reasons of expediency the Radicals were the only ones who opposed him on grounds of doctrine. It is also true, as Professor Donald has again told us, that the Radicals fell in behind Lincoln at the last and worked for his re-election. But they fell in with sullen acquiescence and only because they had no other alternative. As the canny observer who edited the New York *Herald* noted, all the Republican elements had to support Lincoln in the hope of getting something from him:

> Whatever they say now, we venture to predict that Wade and his tail; and Bryant and his tail; and Wendell Phillips and his tail; and Weed, Barney, Chase and their tails; and Winter Davis, Raymond, Opdyke and Forney who have no tails; will all make tracks for Old Abe's plantation, and will soon be found crowing and blowing, and vowing and writhing, and swearing and stumping . . . , declaring that he and he alone, is the hope of the nation, the bugaboo of Jeff Davis, the first of Conservatives, the best of Abolitionists, the purest of patriots, the most gullible of mankind, the easiest President to manage, and the person especially predestined and foreordained by Providence to carry on the war, free the niggers, and give all the faithful a fair share of the spoils.[24]

The election of 1864 illustrates many things, among them the wonderful diversity of American parties and the paradox that the Republicans could be at once divided by an abnormal issue and united by the normal requirements of politics.

The most instructive demonstration of the revolutionary temperament of the Radicals, certainly for the historian, is their endeavor to establish the primacy of Congress in the governmental system. Here, as with other areas of war politics, it is necessary to lay down some initial qualifications. Some Conservative advocated a larger role for Congress in the management of the war, and the Radical push in this direction represented in part the normal reaction of the legislative branch against the executive in a time of crisis. But the Radical leaders proposed to go beyond a defense against executive expansion or even an enlargement of legislative influence. Essentially they wanted to set up a kind of Congressional dictatorship. They would do this formally—some Radicals favored the installation of the English cabinet system[25]—or, preferably, informally, by overshadowing the executive with the power of Congress. The latter course was exemplified notably in the creation and the career of the Committee on the Conduct of the War, a unique agency in our history and undeniably a Radical-dominated body. Ostensibly an investigative mechanism, it attempted to be also and with substantial success a policy-forming institution. The Committee's work cannot be adequately treated here, but in summary it is accurate to say that in no other of our conflicts did Congress attain such a dominant voice in the direction of military affairs.[26]

The lines on the legislature versus the executive issue were drawn early. Just a few months after the war started, Senator Jacob Collamer, speaking for the administration, warned his Radical colleagues: "War is not a business Congress can engineer. It is properly *Executive* business, and the moment Congress passes beyond the line of providing for the wants of the

Government, and [decides] the purposes of the war, to say how it shall be conducted, the whole thing will prove a failure."²⁷ The Radical answer to this thesis came from many sources and most succinctly from Ben Wade: "The President cannot lay down and fix the principles upon which a war shall be conducted. . . . It is for Congress to lay down the rules and regulations by which the Executive shall be governed in conducting a war."²⁸ Examples of the conflict arising from these opposed concepts are many. The most interesting and revealing one is the December, 1862, attempt of the Republican senators to force Lincoln to reform his cabinet by removing Secretary of State William H. Seward.

The Radicals objected to Seward almost from the day he went into the cabinet. Their criticism of him was simple and typical: he had no principles, or the wrong ones, and, ergo, his presence in the government conducted to a listless prosecution of the war and to eventual defeat. This was, of course, the same kind of denunciation thrown by the Radicals at all their opponents, civil and military. Only men of right doctrine should direct the war because men of wrong doctrine would lose it; generals lost battles not because of a lack of generalship but because of a lack of principle. This notion of a relation between principle and military success, this determination to eliminate men without principle fascinated European observers and led them to liken the Radicals to the faction of the Mountain in the French Revolution.²⁹ In December of 1862 the Radicals had abundant reason to question the absence of victory. The armies seemed stalled on all fronts and the bloody defeat of Fredericksburg had shocked the country. At this moment all the frustration and ire of the Radicals fell upon Seward, who was supposed to have a malign and pervasive influence on the President and who in some mysterious way was responsible for the failure of the armies. Three days after Fredericksburg the Republican senators, at the summons of Radical members, met in a secret caucus. The result of this meeting and another on the next day was a decision to send a delegation to Lincoln to urge on him a reconstitution of the cabinet and changes in the military list. In the words of a paper agreed to by the participants, the "theory" of the American system was that the cabinet should be a unit in "political principles"; and it was "unwise and unsafe" to entrust the direction of important operations or separate commands to generals who did not believe in a vigorous prosecution of the war, or, as Wade put it, to officers who had no sympathy with the cause. The committee, composed of seven Radicals and two Conservatives, met with Lincoln in two stormy sessions. What occurred at these gatherings and Lincoln's adroit handling of the situation and his ultimate triumph are too well known to be detailed.[30] The broader meaning of the episode does, however, require notice.

Not even Professor Donald contends that this affair represents the normal workings of American politics. But he does argue that it cannot be viewed as a Radical project or plot, pointing out that the Conservatives participated in the meeting and that all the senators agreed on the sentiments in the paper to be presented to Lincoln. This is, like his thesis on a whole, partially right and partially the opposite; it clarifies our understanding of the episode and at the same time obscures it. The motives of the senators were several and complex. Some of both factions wanted Seward out because they disliked him personally or politically or because they thought he did exert a bad influence on Lincoln. Others, and again of both factions, honestly thought, and with some reason, that Lincoln did not make sufficient use of his cabinet and that an alteration in it might force him to change his procedure. But in the last analysis the December offensive has still to be viewed as a Radical maneuver. It is evident, from Senator Fessenden's account of the event, from Senator Browning's diary, and from other sources,[31] that the Radicals instigated and influenced the caucus and that the

Conservatives went along, if for no other reason, because they had to. They hoped to avoid a factional fight and to soften the resolutions presented to the President; thus whereas the Radicals proposed to demand of Lincoln that he reform the cabinet the Conservatives persuaded the caucus to approve a request for reform. Moreover, in the meetings with Lincoln the Radicals took the lead in denouncing Seward and conservative dominance in the government and the army; and, most significant, they were the only ones who contended, either to the caucus or to the President, that doctrine should be the basis for removing or retaining either civil or military officials. And while many of the senators showed a certain fuzziness about the nature of the governmental system, it was the Radicals who boldly admitted that the Senate was stepping outside its proper sphere. Fessenden told the caucus that the time had arrived when the Senate could no longer "content itself with the discharge of its constitutional duties," and after the affair was over he characterized it as "a new point in history . . . a new proceeding— one probably unknown to the government of the country."[32]

In the constitutional sense the December crisis was in large part an attempt by Congress to extend its control to the appointing and removing power of the executive. In the political sense it was, as Washington observers well realized, a scheme to force Lincoln to reconstitute his cabinet on a Radical basis, with Secretary of the Treasury Salmon P. Chase emerging as the dominating figure. It could have become something entirely different. At the height of the affair, when it seemed that the cabinet might break up, both Radicals and Conservatives descended on Lincoln with proposed slates for his new group of advisers. It has escaped the notice of all commentators that the Conservatives may have supported the original movement because they too had a motive to dissolve the cabinet. Just as the Radicals considered Lincoln to be too close to the Conservatives, so the latter thought him to be too cozy with the Radicals.

The more ultra Conservatives thought that if they could surround him with men of their stamp they could control him. But Lincoln had no intention of falling under the dominance of either faction. He would have neither a completely Radical nor a completely Conservative cabinet. It is highly significant that when he rejected Browning's suggested list of Conservative members he said such a cabinet would "be in his way on the negro question." He meant that in dealing with slavery he would be bound by neither extreme, that he would go neither too fast nor too slow.

Both of the Republican factions were puzzled at times as to which side Lincoln espoused, and so also were more objective observers. "The conservative Republicans think him too much in the hands of the radicals," one reporter noted, "while the radical Republicans think him too slow, yielding, and half-hearted."[33] A Democratic journalist, trying to analyze the conflict in the Republican party, came closer than he perhaps realized to the truth, to the paradox that the Republicans were at once concurrent and contrary. Lincoln was in his beliefs, thought this man, as one with the Radicals. But he was not accepted by them as a leader because he had not done "everything in their particular way, and at their designated moment."[34] Congressman Owen Lovejoy, a Radical without the personal dislike of Lincoln manifested by many Radicals, propounded an identical analysis in more striking language. The President was like a man trying to handle two horses, Lovejoy conjectured. The superb Radical horse wanted to clear all barriers at once, while the poor Conservative horse held back. Lovejoy criticized Lincoln for checking the forward steed but then added: "If he does not drive as fast as I would, he is on the same road, and it is a question of time."[35] These last two comments embody the essence of the paradox and the essence of the Republican division. Lincoln and the Radicals *were* in agreement on the ultimate goal, the extinction of slavery. On the great end there was no fundamental difference between them. But they *were* divided on the method and the timing, on how fast and in what manner they should move toward the goal. Both were committed to bringing about a wrenching social change. One would do it with the experimental caution of the pragmatist, the other with the headlong rush of the doctrinaire. And this matter of method on this particular issue was a fundamental difference. If a question of semantics arises concerning the use of fundamental, it can at least be said that the difference was deeper and darker than the fissures normally separating American political groups. It should not be exaggerated. But it cannot be exorcised.

Lincoln was on the slavery question, as he was on most matters, a conservative. Unlike the ultra Radicals, he could tolerate evil, especially when he feared that to uproot it would produce greater evils. But he was not the kind of conservative who refused to move at all against evil, who let his pragmatism fade into expediency, who blindly rejected change when it could not be denied. Yet there were just such men among the ultra Conservatives of his party, and Lincoln opposed them as he did the ultra Radicals. He knew that he was not completely with them, and, as he told Browning, he would not let the Conservatives control the slavery issue. He knew too that he was against the Radicals and also with them. Speaking of the Missouri Radicals but doubtless having the whole genre in mind, he said: "They are utterly lawless—the unhandiest devils in the world to deal with—but after all their faces are set Zionwards."[36] He did work with the Radicals but he also resisted them. He used them—as he did the Conservatives—to effect a great social change with the smallest possible social dislocation. It would indeed be an error, as we are in Professor Donald's debt for telling us, to make too much out of the conflict in the Republican party over slavery. It would be a greater error to dismiss this unique episode and its unique issue as something normal or average and to treat it on the level of ordinary politics. There is little about the Civil War that is ordinary.

NOTES

1. Joshua F. Speed to Joseph Holt, November 28, December 8, 1861, in Joseph Holt Papers (Library of Congress).

2. Howard K. Beale, ed., *The Diary of Edward Bates* (Washington, 1933), 333, entry of February 13, 1864.

3. Thaddeus Stevens to ————————, November 17, 1862, in Thaddeus Stevens Papers (Library of Congress).

4. *Wilkes' Spirit of the Times* (New York), June 18, 1864.

5. *Congressional Globe,* 38 Cong., 2 Sess., 165.

6. David Donald, *Lincoln Reconsidered* (Vintage Edition; New York, 1961), 103–27.

7. Eric McKitrick, *Andrew Johnson and Reconstruction* (Chicago, 1960), *passim.*

8. *Congressional Globe,* 37 Cong., 1 Sess., 119, 142–43, 189; New York *Evening Post,* December 5, 1861; New York *Times,* December 5, 1861.

9. Roy P. Basler, ed., *The Collected Works of Abraham Lincoln* (Rutgers, 1953), V, 48–49; George W. Julian, *Select Speeches of George W. Julian* (Cincinnati, 1867), 33.

10. The economic beliefs and program of the Radicals are subject to all kinds of semantic analyses. It can be argued, for example, that the Radicals were really radical in that they proposed to overthrow or destroy one of the largest aggregations of property in the country, to execute a gigantic confiscation of private property. The paradox here was, as some of them came to realize, that confiscation would be employed by men who believed in *laissez faire* to strengthen a system that glorified private ownership. Or, to take another approach, while the Radicals customarily cast their attacks on slavery in moral terms, it can be said that to them slavery was a symbol of many things and that within the context of the symbol there were economic facets of which they were perhaps unaware. That is, a Radical may have denounced slavery as a sin without realizing all his motives, one being that the sinners, the slaveholders, prevented an industry in his state from getting tariff protection.

We know a great deal about what the Radicals were against economically and something about what specific measures they were for. But we do not know enough about their image of the economy as a whole. Did they agree or differ as to its structure? Ben Wade once made a speech in Kansas in which he was reported to have advocated some kind of equal division of property. If he said it—Wade denied he had phrased it exactly that way—why did he say it? Do his remarks reveal the zeal of a revolutionary or a radical? Did he have sincere equalitarian instincts? Or was he merely indulging in an oratorical flight that might aid his political ambitions? The entire subject of the Radical concept of economics needs more research before we can generalize broadly.

11. *Congressional Globe,* 38 Cong., 2 Sess., 165.

12. John G. Nicolay and John Hay, *Abraham Lincoln: A History* (New York, 1914), IX, 100.

13. Wendell Phillips to George W. Julian, March 27, 1864, in Giddings-Julian Correspondence (Library of Congress); Theodore C. Smith, *Life and Letters of James A. Garfield* (New Haven, 1925), I, 375; *Wilkes' Spirit of the Times,* January 30, 1864.

14. Joshua R. Giddings to George W. Julian, March 22, 1863, in Giddings-Julian Correspondence; L. Maria Child to Julian, April 8, 1865, *ibid.*

15. *Congressional Globe,* 38 Cong., 2 Sess., 161.

16. New York *Tribune,* May 12, 1863.

17. Edward L. Pierce, *Memoir and Letters of Charles Sumner* (Boston, 1887–93), IV, 142–43. For other similar Radical expressions, see Congressman Charles Sedgwick, in Sarah F. Hughes, ed., *Letters and Recollections of John Murray Forbes* (Boston, 1899), I, 96–7, 321; Horace Greeley to Mrs. Margaret Allen, June 17, 1861, in Horace Greeley Papers (Library of Congress); J. H. Walker to Thaddeus Stevens, February 27, 1864, in Stevens Papers; C. A. Preston to John Sherman, December 1, 1863, in John Sherman Papers (Library of Congress); J. H. Jordan to Lyman Trumbull, February 20, 1862, in Lyman Trumbull Papers (Library of Congress); David Prince to Trumbull, September 16, 1862, *ibid.*

18. New York *Tribune,* January 24, 1863, Stevens to ————, in Stevens Papers, September 5, 1862.

19. *Congressional Globe,* 37 Cong., 1 Sess., 75; *ibid.,* 37 Cong., 3 Sess., 1338.

20. New York *Tribune,* September 11, 1862; *Congressional Globe,* 37 Cong., 2 Sess., 1896.

21. T. Harry Williams, *Lincoln and the Radicals* (Madison, 1941), 14–17.

22. *Wilkes' Spirit of the Times,* January 30, 1864.

23. The election of 1864 is treated in Williams, *Lincoln and the Radicals,* Chapter 12.

24. New York *Herald,* August 24, 1864.

25. *Frank Leslie's Illustrated Newspaper* (New York), October 31, 1863.

26. For the organization and work of the Committee, see Williams, *Lincoln and the Radicals,* Chapter 3.

27. Washington *National Intelligencer,* December 6, 1861.

28. *Congressional Globe,* 37 Cong., 2 Sess., 1918.

29. London *Times,* quoted in Detroit *Free Press,* January 23, 1863.

30. Williams, *Lincoln and the Radicals,* 208–11; Allan Nevins, *The War for the Union, II, War Becomes Revolution* (New York, 1960), 352–62.

31. Francis Fessenden, *Life and Public Services of William Pitt Fessenden* (Boston, 1901), I, 231–51; Theodore C. Pease and James G. Randall, eds., *The Diary of Orville Hickman Browning* (Springfield, 1925), I, 596–604.

32. Fessenden, *Fessenden,* I, 233–34, 253; *Harper's Weekly* (New York), January 3, 1863.

33. *Harper's Weekly,* August 29, 1863, "Lounger's" column.

34. Springfield *Illinois State Register,* January 13, 1863, quoted in A.C.

Cole, "President Lincoln and the Illinois Radical Republicans," *Mississippi Valley Historical Review,* IV (March, 1918), 427.

35. New York *Tribune,* June 13, 1862.

36. Tyler Dennett, ed., *Lincoln and the Civil War in the Diaries of John Hay* (New York, 1939), 108.